CHRISTIAN, YES — BUT WHY CATHOLIC?

Helpful Ideas on Explaining & Defending Your Faith

Rev. Joseph M. Esper

PUBLISHING COMPANY
P.O. Box 220 • Goleta, CA 93116
(800) 647-9882 • (805) 692-0043 • Fax: (805) 967-5133
www.queenship.org

Library of Congress Number # 2007930516

Published by:
    Queenship Publishing
    P.O. Box 220
    Goleta, CA 93116
    (800) 647-9882 • (805) 692-0043 • Fax: (805) 967-5133
    www.queenship.org

Printed in the United States of America

ISBN: 978-1-57918-340-9

Dedicated
to the
Immaculate Heart of Mary

CHRISTIAN, YES, BUT WHY CATHOLIC?
Authored by
Reverend Joseph Esper

IMPRIMATUR

His Eminence, Adam Cardinal Maida
Archbishop of Detroit

Given in Detroit, Michigan, on April 25, 2007

NIHIL OBSTAT

Reverend Monsignor John P. Zenz, S.T.L.
Censor deputatis

Given in Detroit, Michigan, on April 24, 2007

TABLE OF CONTENTS

FOREWORD

St. Peter tells us, "Always be ready to give an explanation to anyone who asks you for a reason for your hope" (1 Pt. 3:15). Our hope, of course, is in Jesus Christ, and in the gift of salvation He offers us through His Holy Catholic Church.

Many Christians of other denominations find our hope baffling or even incomprehensible. "How can you be a *Catholic?*," they ask. "Why do you settle for meaningless, confusing rituals and man-made traditions, when instead you should be relying solely upon God's Word in Scripture, the way we do?" (Some Fundamentalists and other "Bible Christians" will be even more blunt and accusatory: "Why are you throwing away your chance of salvation by remaining enslaved to the 'Whore of Babylon?'") Most of us have encountered such questions and challenges, expressed with varying degrees of politeness (perhaps even by loved ones genuinely concerned over the state of our souls). What answer should we give? What defense of Catholicism should we make?

When we explain our Faith, St. Peter advises, "Do it with gentleness and reverence, keeping your conscience clear, so that, when you are maligned, those who defame your good conduct in Christ may themselves be put to shame" (1 Pt. 3:16). The Church expects us to defend and explain our Catholic beliefs when necessary—and so this requires an adult understanding and experience of the Faith on our part. Unfortunately, not all the Church's members have been willing or able to meet this standard.

Over the years, I've become very tired of reading about or hearing former Catholics say, "When I belonged to the Catholic Church, I really didn't know Jesus, but now that I'm a member of my new (non-Catholic) church, I've accepted Him as my Lord and Savior," or "When I used to be Catholic, we never really studied Scripture, but now I've found everything I need in the Bible." While being glad for their deeper love for the Lord (and also not wanting to question their sincerity), I can't help but think of such persons as "modern day Esaus" (cf. Gen. 25:33), willing to give away their Catholic birthright and the ability to receive Jesus Himself in the Holy Eucharist (something of immense value available only to Catholics).

As my own admittedly limited, but heartfelt, response to this situation, I devised a simple junior high course on introductory apologetics (which I use with our students every year); later, I expanded it into a well-received adult education series for use in my parish. One of the parishioners in attendance thanked me afterwards, saying she only wished her own grown children could have heard something like this when they were receiving instructions in their Catholic Faith (back in the era when catechesis was largely "content free"). This book—based on the adult education series I presented—is offered in response to this need.

There are numerous contemporary books available on Catholic apologetics—including many by recent converts to Catholicism—and these do a fine job explaining and defending the Church's teachings and practices. (Some of the best of them are given in the Recommended Reading list.) This work is certainly not intended to replace or improve upon them, but it is designed to be a useful supplement; while some overlapping with other books will occur (especially in the chapters giving a Catholic understanding of important scriptural passages), I've tried to tie together and present some useful (and, I believe, very interesting) ideas that normally aren't considered when Catholic followers of Christ are required to defend their Faith.

The title of this book comes from an apologetics article I once wrote for *This Rock* magazine, and is re-used with their permission. (The article is also the source of the material in chapter 5.)

Many Catholics are afraid of the idea of apologetics, feeling that while they *know* their Faith is true, they're unable to do a very good job explaining *why*. It's my hope this short book will serve as a useful reference (and point them toward other even better works on this subject), while providing them with a greater awareness and appreciation of what it means to be a Catholic in today's world.

> Rev. Joseph M. Esper
> August 22, 2006
> Feast of the Queenship of Mary

SEARCHING
FOR THE TRUTH

Chapter 1:

Introduction

In the 2nd century a Greek philosopher named Athenagoras not only doubted the truth of Christianity, but was determined to disprove it. In order to know what he was attacking, he first thoroughly studied this fairly new religion—and ended up becoming Catholic himself. Athenagoras had originally planned to write a philosophical attack on Christianity, but found himself "captured" by its beauty and coherence; as a result, he wound up writing an elaborated explanation and defense of it instead.

Something similar happened in 19th century England. Many members of the Anglican church, such as John Henry Newman, were becoming Catholic; the British Freemasons—who bitterly opposed Catholicism—decided to fight this trend. They appointed their Grand Master, the highly-educated Marquis of Ripon, to write a book debunking the teachings and authority of the Church. Like Athenagoras 1700 years earlier, he studied Catholicism in order to know what he was attacking—and ten months later he asked to be received into the Church. When the priest he approached expressed surprise at his request, the Marquis responded, "I came upon three things in the Catholic Church whereby every unbiased person must see that this Church, and only this one, is the Church of Jesus Christ. In the Catholic Church is the rock, the confessional, and the tabernacle."

The many people who've freely entered the Church over the centuries are a living and historical testimony to her possession of the truth; the same thing is also true of those who've remained in the Church in spite of terrible persecution and hardship. Catholicism was established in Japan in the 16th century, but before long it was subjected to a fierce persecution. In 1708 the last Catholic priest in Japan, a Jesuit, was martyred, and the authorities—who completely closed off the country from any foreign influences, allowing no one to enter or leave—were convinced that Christianity would soon die out. However, even without any of the sacraments except Baptism, the Japanese Catholics held onto their faith. In 1859, six years after Commodore Matthew Perry led his ships into Tokyo Bay, a treaty opened Japan to foreign commerce and allowed missionaries to return to Japan. A small Catholic chapel was built in Nagasaki, and soon afterwards a group of Japanese from a distant village visited the French priest stationed there. After seeing the chapel, they asked him three questions: "Do you honor the Mother of God? Are you unmarried? Is the Holy Father in Rome the head of your Church?" When the priest answered "yes" to all three questions, they said, "Truly God has sent you to us. We believe the same as you do, and in our village everyone is a Catholic, just as we are."

For simple Japanese Catholics to have preserved their faith for over 150 years without the sacraments (save Baptism, which lay persons can administer), without contact with fellow believers, and surrounded by a hostile culture, was nothing short of miraculous—and completely unexplainable from a worldly perspective. There's something about Catholicism that transcends, or rises above, mere human standards. The world thinks in terms of avoiding pain and sacrifice, and experiencing pleasure and success—but those Japanese Catholics, and tens of millions of other persecuted Christians throughout the centuries, have a different set of values. The world looks for short-term advantages, but we're called to have a much longer perspective.

A sign of true wisdom is our ability to keep our ultimate destiny ever in mind. The 18th century French philosopher Voltaire was a fierce enemy of the Church, and during his final illness a nurse was hired to assist him. From then on, whenever someone wanted to engage her to care for a dying person, she always refused unless the person was a devout Christian—for she said that watching an unbeliever die was such a terrible experience that she never wanted to repeat it.

Christians have reason to face death with hope; this is especially true of Catholics. A physician named Oliver Wendell Holmes—better known as a U.S. Supreme Court justice—was once asked by a minister his opinion, as a doctor, on what religious belief was most helpful to dying persons. He answered, "So far as I have observed persons nearing the end of life, the Roman Catholics understand the business of dying better than Protestants. I have seen a good many Roman Catholics on their dying beds, and it always appeared to me that they accepted the inevitable with the composure which showed that their belief, whether or not the best to live by, was a better one to die by than most of the harder ones that have replaced it."

This testimony from a medical point of view is true in more ways than one. Once a bishop was questioning young people in a confirmation class, and he asked, "What do we mean when we speak of 'false doctrine'?" One boy raised his hand and answered, "It's when the doctor gives the wrong medicine to people who are sick." In a spiritual sense, there's a lot of "false doctoring" going on today, with young people and older persons being led astray by the secular values of our world, and by non-Christian religions, atheism, religious cults, and the New Age Movement. Even other Christian denominations, whose leaders and members are by and large sincere and devout, and presumably personally pleasing to God, can and do fall prey to false beliefs and ideas. Protestants often have major disagreements among themselves on such key issues as salvation and the necessity of baptism—and in spite of these disagreements, each of the many thousands of different denominations claims its beliefs and practices are based on Scripture. With all these confusing contradictions, it's very easy to get a wrong diagnosis and prescription. Only the Catholic Church can claim to be the true Doctor of souls, because only Catholicism can trace its authority back to Jesus Himself—and only Catholics have access to the sure "medicine for sin" provided by the rock of Peter and the Sacraments of the confessional and the tabernacle.

Chapter 2:

Why So Many Conversions?

Every year large numbers of people convert and become Catholic. Many of them were never baptized, and may have belonged to a different non-Christian religion, or no religion at all. There are also quite a few, however, who were baptized in a different Christian denomination, but who now wish to join the Catholic faith. This is true throughout the world, especially in places like Africa, where the Church is experiencing her highest rate of growth; there is also a large number of conversions to Catholicism in the United States—some 200,000 persons each year.

What's especially interesting and encouraging is just the quantity of converts, but the quality: some of Protestantism's most intelligent, dedicated, and sincere pastors, theologians, and lay people are becoming Catholic. (This is probably one of the best-kept secrets of contemporary Christianity here in America.[1]) There are numerous stories of devout, committed Protestants who felt something was missing in their experience of religion, or that their own church's beliefs and practices were inconsistent or incomplete, and who were honest and courageous enough to admit it. Instead of continuing to rely on what other people had told them about the differences between various religions, they prayed for the Holy Spirit's guidance and began studying the Bible and early Church history for themselves—and found to their surprise (and sometimes dismay and *shock*) that the Catholic teaching is the correct one.

Contemporary Catholic authors such as Scott and Kimberly Hahn, Marcus Grodi, Steve Wood, Al Kresta, and Fr. Richard John Neuhaus (a Lutheran minister who became a Catholic priest after his conversion) are just a few examples of Protestant leaders who "crossed the Tiber" and joined the Catholic Church. Many of them had always been convinced that Catholicism was corrupt or mistaken in its beliefs, and that becoming Catholic was a betrayal of the Gospel—and they would have been horrified to learn that they would one day become Catholic themselves. They had to make big sacrifices when they entered the Catholic Church; quite often their Protestant families and friends couldn't understand their decision, and sometimes rejected them. These new Catholics often entered a local church or parish where the preaching, music, and sense of community were weaker than what they were used to in their former denominations, and those of them who were Protestant ministers lost their jobs when they became Catholic. All these converts were willing to undergo these difficulties because the Holy Spirit had shown them beyond any shadow of doubt that the fullness of Christ's Church is to be found only within Catholicism—and they knew that only by becoming Catholic themselves would they truly be at home.

One example involves a former Protestant minister in Detroit named Rev. Alex Jones, who was pastor of Maranatha Christian Church. For 40 years he was on an ongoing search for truth, studying the teachings of virtually every Christian denomination and trying to understand how so many different churches could all claim to be faithful to Jesus Christ, while having so many radically different interpretations of the Bible. Rev. Jones realized that, in order to find the truth, it's not enough just to read the New Testament; after all, every Christian group does that—but their teachings are so different, they can't all be correct. No, he reasoned, to understand the true meaning of the New Testament, it's necessary to learn how the early Christians themselves interpreted it—for if someone had introduced a false or mistaken idea, the original apostles would have still been around to correct it.

Accordingly, Rev. Jones began studying the writings of the Apostolic Fathers—the earliest Church leaders—and he came to realize, to his surprise, that the Catholic Church has indeed faithfully preserved the original Gospel of Jesus Christ. As he noted, "I discovered the word 'tradition.' All my life, I'd been taught that was a bad word, but the early Christians were very concerned about this." He began sharing this shocking but compelling information with others, while modeling his parish's style of worship on the Catholic Mass—and at Easter in 2001, he and one-third of his congregation were formally received into the Catholic Church. As he later stated, "The Christian faith began to grow well beyond the pages of the New Testament. Customs, practices, traditions—all practiced and recognized by the apostles—guided the first-century Church through its formative years. Without knowledge and familiarity with *all* of the Church's teachings, the Protestant grasp of the Christian message may be good, but it is certainly not complete."[2]

There are other similar instances of wholesale conversion; for instance, some Episcopalian parishes here in the United States—including both pastors and their congregations—have voted to become Catholic (and, in a few cases, these Episcopalian priests, though married, were then ordained as Catholic priests). Lifelong Catholics may have difficulty imagining just what a challenging, frightening and even heart-breaking—while at the same time joyous and liberating—experience this type of conversion can be; to leave behind the faith of one's parents and childhood, along with a style of worship and prayer that's often very familiar and comforting, is quite frequently a major sacrifice and a leap of faith. Such Christians are indeed following Our Lord's command to "put out into deep water" (Lk. 5:4), and they deserve the admiration and respect of every Catholic, along with our sincere and ongoing efforts to make them feel welcome in our parishes (an area in which we've often fallen short). Furthermore, the numerous stories of other Christians converting to Catholicism should give us a deeper gratitude and appreciation for our Catholic faith, and a greater willingness and desire to share it with all who are searching for the Truth.

Chapter 3:

Discovering the Truth

Conversions to Catholicism are not just a recent event; they've been occurring for many years. Most of the original Protestants back in the 16th century chose to leave the Catholic Church (though some of them were tricked or forced into doing so); today, however, most Protestants belong to their particular denomination only because they were raised in it and their parents and grandparents belonged to it—so it's not surprising that when they find something better in the Catholic Church, they're willing to convert.

It's possible to discover the truth, however, not only by seeing what the Catholic Church is, but also by seeing what she is not. This was the experience of a great British scholar and author named G. K. Chesterton. He was not a Catholic by birth, but he was very intelligent and capable of brilliant reasoning. He noticed that the Church was always being criticized by all sorts of people—and that their criticisms contradicted each other. People complained that the Church was too old-fashioned. . . or too modern; too strict and demanding . . . or too lenient; too conservative . . . or too liberal; too involved in this world . . . or too other-worldly and spiritual. Chesterton knew all these opposite claims couldn't be true, since they were contradictory; therefore, where was the truth to be found? The most likely place, he realized, was right in the middle—the exact spot occupied by the Church. Chesterton continued to read and study and reflect, and as a result, he became a Catholic in 1922, and spent the rest of his life writing powerful and insightful books and articles defending the Catholic faith.

Catholic evangelist Patrick Madrid edited a book titled *Surprised by Truth,* in which a number of former Protestants described their faith journeys and the reasons why they felt compelled to enter the Catholic Church.[1] Their comments are very enlightening, and some of them are worth examining here:

One convert wrote, "I was . . . compelled by the holiness I found in the lives of the Catholic saints I read about. Many Protestants I knew or had read about were good Christians, but their spirituality and heroic virtues simply couldn't compare with the likes of Francis of Assisi, Teresa of Avila, or Augustine. And although the Catholic saints were very different from each other in temperament, learning, and spirituality, they had one thing in common. All were convinced that the Catholic Church was the only true Church. I reasoned that if these great Christian men and women believed this, it was very likely true."[2]

Another convert explains, "I found the Catholic Church has always held and proclaimed (more clearly and vigorously than any Protestant denomination, I felt), key biblical doctrines such as the inspiration and inerrancy of Scripture, the atonement of Christ, salvation by grace alone, and the need to pursue holiness. . . . Since my conversion many Protestants have asked me, 'Why Catholicism?' I answer: 'Because it is the truth—the fullness of Christian faith; and because in it I can receive the sacraments, Christ's means of imparting grace through the ministry of His Church."[3]

Still another convert wrote, "I kept an open mind and a teachable heart as I studied Scripture alongside these Catholic works. . . . I was amazed at how compelling the biblical and historical case for Catholicism was—how unanswerable its claims were—and as my understanding of Catholicism grew, my respect for it grew also. . . . The Catholic Church seemed to have everything so well thought out—it was a marvelously complex and consistent belief system unparalleled by anything I have ever encountered in Evangelicalism."[4] This former Protestant also noted, "I was falling prey to Chesterton's principle of conversion: that one cannot examine Catholicism and not develop an admiration for it—an admiration that almost invariably leads to becoming convinced of its truth."[5]

Studying the writings of the Church Fathers played an important role in the conversion of one former Protestant: "During my Calvary Chapel days I had a very low view of the sacraments; I was almost anti-sacramental. But when I discovered the true role of baptism and the Lord's Supper in Christian worship and living, a corresponding appreciation for the role of the Church began to blossom. That's when I did something really dangerous. I started reading the early Church Fathers firsthand. I had studied some early Church history, but too much of it was from perspectives limited by Protestant history textbooks. I was shocked to discover in the writings of the first-, second-, and third-century Christians a very high view of the Church and liturgy, very much unlike the views of the typical Evangelical Protestant. The worship and government of the early Church didn't look anything like the things I saw at Calvary Chapel or my own congregation. It looked a lot more, well, Catholic."[6]

One former fundamentalist converted to Catholicism in part because of the Church's heavy reliance on the Bible during worship. He sought to find a way of comparing the use of Scripture by various denominations; as he writes, "I tried to come up with some objective method of measuring the feelings of different churches for the Bible and what it says. I decided to time the percentage of Sunday morning worship spent in Scripture reading in three different types of churches." As it turned out, the Evangelical church he visited spent less than 6% of its worship service actually reading, singing, or reciting Scripture; a fundamentalist church used the Bible for only 2% of the service he attended. In contrast, he writes, "Catholics at Mass spend more than 26% of the time in Scripture."[7]

In spite of Catholicism's profound respect for Scripture, some bitterly anti-Catholic fundamentalists accuse the Catholic Church of being the "whore of Babylon," the evil woman mentioned in the Book of Revelation (17:1-6) as a symbol of wickedness. However, it was studying Revelation that helped one leading Protestant biblical scholar, Dr. Scott Hahn, become convinced of the truth of Catholicism. In his book *The Lamb's Supper* he writes:

> There I stood, a man incognito, a Protestant minister in plainclothes, slipping into the back of a Catholic chapel in Milwaukee to witness my first Mass. Curiosity had driven me there, and I still didn't feel sure it was *healthy* curiosity. Studying the writings of the earliest Christians, I'd found countless references to "the liturgy," "the Eucharist," "the sacrifice." For those first Christians, the Bible — the book I loved above all — was incomprehensible apart from the event that today's Catholics called "the Mass" . . . For years, as an evangelical Calvinist, I'd been trained to believe that the Mass was the ultimate sacrilege a human could commit. The Mass, I had been taught, was a ritual that purported to "resacrifice Jesus Christ." So I would remain an observer. I would stay seated, with my Bible open beside me.
>
> As the Mass moved on, however, something hit me. My Bible wasn't just beside me. It was before me — *in the words of the Mass!* One line was from Isaiah, another from the Psalms, another from Paul. The experience was overwhelming. I wanted to stop everything and shout, "Hey, can I explain what's happening from Scripture? This is great!"[8]

Dr. Hahn returned to Mass the next day, and the day after that — and each time he recognized more of the Scriptures being fulfilled before his eyes. The most vividly-portrayed scriptural work of all, however, was the Book of Revelation; moreover, he discovered for himself what the early Church Fathers knew: the Catholic Mass is the key to interpreting and understanding Revelation's meaning.

As noted in *The Lamb's Supper*, only the Catholic Church has all the elements of heavenly worship described in the Book of Revelation: Sunday worship (1:10), a high priest (1:13), an altar (8:3-4; 11:1; 14:18); priests (*presbyteroi*) (4:4; 11:15; 14:3; 19:4); vestments (1:13; 4:4; 6:11; 7:9; 15:6; 19:13-14); consecrated celibacy (14:4); penitence (chapters 2 & 3); incense (5:8; 8:3-5); the book, or scroll (5:1); the Eucharistic Host (2:17); chalices (15:7; chapter 16; 21:9); the Sign of the Cross (the *tau*) (7: 3; 14:1; 22:4); the Gloria (15:3-4); the Alleluia (19:1,3,4,6); "Lift up your hearts" (11:12); the "Holy, Holy, Holy" (4:8); the Amen (19:4; 22:21); the "Lamb of God" (5:6 and throughout); the prominence of the Virgin Mary (12:1-6,13-17); intercession of angels and saints (5:8; 6:9-10; 8:3-4); devotion to St. Michael the Archangel (12:7); antiphonal chant (4:8-11; 5:9-14; 7:10-12; 18:1-8); readings from Scripture (chapters 2, 3, & 5; 8:2-11); the priesthood of the faithful (1:6; 20:6); catholicity, or universality (7:9); silent contemplation (8:1), and the marriage supper of the Lamb (19:9,17).[9]

These are only a few of the many testimonies given by ex-Protestants as to why they became Catholic; again and again, people have discovered the religious truths and spiritual treasures we as Catholics so often take for granted.

Chapter 4:

The Enemy's Testimony

Common sense, and the observations of our own eyes, tell us that human beings make mistakes all the time, and that they don't like having their errors pointed out to them. St. John's Gospel tells us that when the light of Christ came into the world, "men loved darkness instead of light because their deeds were evil" (3:9). Jesus was rejected by many people in His day because He insisted they repent of their sins, and they didn't want to; therefore, it's logical to assume His true Church would also be the target of hatred, criticism, and misunderstanding.

The great Catholic author and Church leader Archbishop Fulton J. Sheen (d. 1979) wrote, "[If I were looking for the truth,] I would begin my search by looking through the world for a Church that did not get along with the evil in the world! If that Church [were] accused of countless lies, hated because it refused to compromise, ridiculed because it refused to fit the times . . . I would suspect that since it was hated by what is evil in the world, it therefore was good and holy; and if good and holy, it must be Divine."

One way of determining which is the true religion or Church is to ask which one has suffered the most. Jesus called Satan "the prince of this world" (Jn. 12:31), and as such, the devil can be expected to oppose and attack any religious movement which threatens his kingdom of evil— and he will reserve his fiercest assaults for what he sees as his biggest threats. Therefore, we can ask: Which religions have been the most persecuted since the time of Christ? The answer is simple: Judaism and Catholicism.

The Jews were God's Chosen People, to whom He promised to send a Savior for the entire world. Most of the Jews rejected Jesus, but according to St. Paul, they remain very precious to God, and eventually will recognize Jesus as their Messiah (Rm. 11:25ff). The Jews have suffered terribly throughout history, sometimes even at the hands of so-called Christians; the Nazis' murder of six million Jews during World War II was by far the worst, but by no means the only, persecution they've experienced. Because God loves the Jewish people so much, Satan hates them intensely. The devil also hates the Catholic Church, more than any other, for she is the one Christian religion directly founded by Christ; St. Paul even refers to the Church as the true "Israel of God" (Gal. 6:16), for she fulfills the role God had originally intended for the Jews.

In our society today, it's politically incorrect to criticize or attack the Jewish people (and that's a good thing), but there are two religious groups who are criticized, ridiculed, and scorned all the time: Bible-believing Christians, whom we might call Fundamentalists, Evangelicals, and Pentecostals; and Catholics. These are the groups most active in speaking out against abortion and euthanasia; these are the groups least willing to compromise with the false values of the world; these are the groups making the greatest efforts to transform society by evangelizing and preaching the Gospel—and for all these reasons, these are the most frequent targets of the news media and entertainment industry.

The Catholic Church in particular is constantly mocked, criticized, and condemned by her enemies—and this is a strong indication that she has Satan worried. The devil sees and understands things that are hidden from most people; he knows who his strongest enemy is. Bible Christians are paying a heavy price for trying to follow Christ faithfully, and they deserve our admiration and support—but that doesn't mean they have the fullness of the Christian message. Only the Catholic Church preaches the Gospel in all its richness, and that's why Satan hates her more than any other religion—but as Jesus promised, the Church will be victorious (Mt. 16:18).

Signs of this coming triumph over evil, and of the Adversary's efforts to prevent it, have been present throughout much of history. For instance, as most Catholics know, the Virgin Mary appeared to St. Bernadette outside the small French town of Lourdes in 1858. What isn't commonly known is that the devil attempted to interfere with these visions, causing, for instance, annoying and distracting noises, and shouting "Flee! Flee!" until quieted by a commanding glance from Our Lady. Moreover, Satan instigated at least fifty false apparitions in the area over the following few years in an effort to discredit the messages given to St. Bernadette (messages eventually accepted as authentic by the Church).[1]

Many of Catholic saints had first-hand experiences of the devil's hatred for the Church, including St. Anthony of Egypt in the 4th century, St. Rose of Lima in the 17th century, and St. Pio of Pietrelcina (Padre Pio) in the 20th century. The holy French priest known as Cure d'Ars, St. John Vianney, was frequently beaten or otherwise harassed by the devil; this was a testimony to the fruitfulness of the saint's ministry, for it frequently meant that a particularly notorious sinner was about to come to St. John for confession. (Indeed, the devil is said to have complained that if there were three other priests in the world such as the Cure d' Ars, his kingdom would be destroyed.)

Jesus has entrusted some powerful spiritual weapons to His Church, and the saints made good use of them. St. John Vianney, for instance, repelled the devil's attacks with the Sign of the Cross; St. Rita of Cascia used this same ritual to release a woman who had been demonically possessed for many years.[2] On several occasions, St. Paul of the Cross brought relief to persons suffering demonic assaults by placing a rosary around their necks. A favorite weapon of St. Teresa of Avila was holy water; as she explained, "I have learned from long experience that there is nothing like holy water to put devils to flight and prevent them from coming back again. They also flee from the Cross, but return; so holy water must have great virtue."[3]

Perhaps the greatest scourge of the devil is the Eucharist. As recorded in *The Mystical City of God*, Our Lady revealed to Ven. Mary of Agreda:

> Lucifer and his demons have such a fear of the most Holy Eucharist, that to approach it causes them more torments than to remain in hell itself. Although they do enter churches in order to tempt souls, they enter them with aversion, forcing themselves to endure cruel pains in hope of destroying a soul and drawing it into sin, especially in holy places and in the presence of the Holy Eucharist. Nothing except their furious hatred of the Lord and against souls could ever induce them to expose themselves to the torments of His real sacramental presence. . . .[4]

Our Lord stated that Satan, the ruler of this world, has no power over Him (Jn. 14:31)—and it stands to reason that His Church will also possess a very real authority over evil. Thus, in an unintended and unwilling way, the devil himself—through his hatred, opposition, and aversion to the Church's sacraments, rituals, and sacramentals—testifies to the power and truth of Catholicism.

Chapter 5:

Ten Reasons for Being (or Becoming) Catholic

The Church's experience of the world's hostility and the devil's hatred gives eloquent testimony that Catholicism is faithfully following in her Master's footsteps, for as Jesus warned, "If they persecuted Me, they will also persecute you" (Jn. 15:20). The fierce opposition encountered by the Church can be considered an indirect compliment to her effectiveness in proclaiming the Gospel. Many people, however, might be looking for more positive reasons to remain or become Catholic. Here are ten:

1. **Only through the Catholic Church can Christians trace their roots back to Christ Himself.**[1] The Acts of the Apostles tells us that within a few short years of the Resurrection of Jesus, His followers began calling themselves "Christians" (11:26), and by the end of the 1st century, the word "catholic"—meaning universal—was applied to the Church. The idea of Christianity dividing into different (and often competing) denominations would have been unthinkable to the 1st century followers of Christ, especially in light of His reference to one shepherd and one flock (Jn. 10:15) and His prayer that His disciples remain one (Jn. 17:22). It was only human weakness that brought about such religious divisions. The Orthodox Church separated from Rome in 1054, and the various Protestant denominations date back no earlier than the 16th century; these Christians can trace their roots back to Christ only through the Catholic Church. That being the case, why should we settle for imitations when the original is available?

2. **The Eucharist and the Real Presence of Christ can truly be found in the Catholic Church.** In chapter 6 of St. John's Gospel, Jesus describes Himself as the bread of life, and states very clearly and forcefully that that whoever eats His flesh and drinks His blood will have eternal life (6:54). Furthermore, at the Last Supper He gave the apostles and their successors, the bishops (and, through them, validly ordained priests), the power and authority to continue to make present His sacrifice when He said "Do this in memory of Me" (Lk. 22:19). Only Catholic (and Orthodox) priests can claim to have been ordained through this line of apostolic succession, and therefore only they

have the sacramental power to consecrate the Eucharist. Moreover, most other Christian denominations understand the Eucharist in incomplete or symbolic terms—not as the true Body, Blood, Soul, and Divinity of Christ, as proclaimed by Catholicism. No Catholic who truly understands the value and importance of the Eucharist would ever consider becoming a "modern-day Esau" (cf. Gen. 25:33-34) by relinquishing his or her spiritual birthright as a member of Christ's true Church, for Holy Communion—a gift available only in the Catholic Church—is truly a "pearl of great price" (cf. Mt. 13:46) worth every sacrifice.

3. **Unlike many other Christians, Catholics have a fully sacramental understanding of God's saving activity.** This refers not only to the seven sacraments, but—in a larger sense—to the Church's recognition that God can be known and experienced through His creation. Catholicism celebrates and encourages our use of the talents and abilities the Lord has given; the Church's historic patronage of the arts and promotion of education is but one example of this. Because human beings are both body and soul, the Lord relates to us not only in an invisible, spiritual way, but also through the use of human gestures and material items we can see, hear, touch, and taste: bread, water, wine, oil, words, the imposition of hands, colors, and so on—all of which are found in the seven sacraments of the Church (and which Catholicism alone has preserved).

4. **Because of the Church's *magisterium* (teaching authority), Catholics have the assurance that their beliefs are divinely-revealed truths, not human interpretations and opinions.** It's said there are now over *27,000* different Protestant denominations (many of them being only the size of a store-front church), all with their own—often contradictory—interpretation of the Gospel, and each claiming *its* interpretation of the Bible is correct. This is obviously impossible, for God is a God of order and truth, not of contradiction and uncertainty. The fact that human beings can easily fall into such divisions and confusion proves the need for some ultimate authority to decide on the proper interpretation of Scripture. Jesus came to proclaim God's truth (Jn. 18:37), and He entrusted this same teaching authority to His Church (Lk. 10:16). The Church was built on the

solid foundation of fidelity and truth (Mt. 7:24-25) and on the rock of Peter's faith (Mt. 16:18-19). This authority also serves as a source and measure of unity—something sorely lacking in Protestantism.

5. **The Catholic Church, more than any other, gives fitting honor to the Mother of God.** Contrary to what some Protestants believe, we do not "worship" Mary (for God alone deserves our worship and adoration), but we do give her the highest possible honor—and in so doing, we are being true to Scripture. The Hail Mary quotes the words of the angel Gabriel (Lk. 1:28), and Mary herself had, under the inspiration of the Holy Spirit, prophesied that "all ages will call me blessed" (Lk. 1:48). The Catholic Church is virtually unique in obeying and fulfilling this prophecy. Moreover, it is only right that we honor her, for one of the commandments says, "Honor your father and mother" (Ex. 20:12). If God wants us to honor our own mothers, He certainly wants us—as Catholicism so richly understands—to honor *His* Mother.

6. **More than any other religion, Catholicism takes Scripture seriously.** This assertion may surprise those who believe Catholics are ignorant of Scripture, and that the only true Bible Christians are Protestants. However, it was the Catholic Church that, under the inspiration of the Holy Spirit, created the Bible as we know it (compiling the books of the Old Testament and writing those of the New Testament), and it was the Church that decided which of the many early Christian writings were canonical, or worthy of acceptance as Scripture. (Indeed, Protestant Bibles actually depend upon the authority of the Catholic Church in this regard.) Moreover, none of the Church's teachings and practices contradict Scripture, and the Bible—either directly or indirectly—supports all the Church's doctrines. Catholicism believes in *everything* the Bible contains, including doctrines often ignored or rejected by Protestants: Christ's teaching on the Eucharist (Jn. 6), the authority of Peter (Mt. 16:18-19), and the forgiveness of sins (Jn. 20:22-23).

7. **The Church has survived and even thrived for 2000 years in spite of every form of persecution, opposition, and difficulty.** As Jesus promised (Mt. 16:18), the gates of Hell have not prevailed against

the Church. Satan has attacked her by means of persecution, heresy, schism, anti-popes, wars, false prophets, civil disturbances, natural disasters, plagues, barbarian invasion, and societal collapse—but the Church always survives these attacks, and becomes even stronger. No less a persecutor of the Church than Napoleon Bonaparte observed, "The nations of the earth pass away, and thrones fall to the ground; the Church alone remains." Even the foolish, incompetent, and sometimes downright evil leadership of certain popes, bishops, and priests, and the moral failings or spiritual indifference of many lay persons, hasn't prevented destroyed the Church or caused her to abandon her mission. Such miraculous preservation can only be explained by the saving presence and activity of the Holy Spirit.

8. **Of all Christian religions, Catholicism has the most accurate and complete understanding of human nature.** This is true particularly in the areas of *reconciliation, ritual,* and *role models.* In terms of reconciliation, the Church recognizes that being saved from our sins is an ongoing process, and not something that happens only once, as many Evangelical Protestants suggest (and that's why the Church has a Sacrament to forgive sins committed after Baptism). In regard to ritual, sociology teaches that recognizable and shared customs are a necessary and inherent part of human culture, and the Church helps meet such needs (as with her ceremonies and rites, and such things as the Sign of the Cross, genuflections, and blessings with holy water, among others). Role models are often of vital importance for personal human development, especially among the young—and Catholicism, more than any other religion, provides and emphasizes such models in the saints.

9. **Catholicism reflects the nature of Heaven more accurately than any other religion.** Like Heaven, with its nine choirs of angels, each having its own function and rank, the Church has a hierarchical structure—and yet, all her members are fundamentally equal. Also, the Church is universal; Catholics are found in virtually every nation, culture, and social status; this parallels Heaven, whose citizenship consists of "a great multitude, which no one could count, of every nation, race, people, and tongue" (Rev. 7:9). Last, all members of the Church are united as one, while preserving their individuality—a

reality that's perfectly experienced in Heaven, where each person is completely absorbed in contemplating God's Divine Majesty, and yet more fully alive and unique than ever before.

10. Because she is rooted in, but also transcends, time and history, the Church is able to help her members discover and live by God's unchanging truth. Other Christian religions have changed some of their teachings (e.g., most Protestants have abandoned the Reformers' condemnation of birth control). Also, some denominations—when too closely identified with a particular nation or culture—may be unduly influenced by politics or popular opinion. The Catholic Church, because of her international presence and prestige, is a powerful political force in her own right, as demonstrated by Pope John Paul II's vital role in the collapse of the Soviet empire and the liberation of Eastern Europe. Church officials are often able to work behind the scenes in mediating conflicts and defending the rights of the oppressed, while remaining true to the Church's other-worldly mission. Jesus prayed that His disciples would be consecrated to the truth, for they are in the world but not of the world (Jn. 17:11-18). Through the Catholic Church, His prayer continues to be fulfilled.

PROTESTANT CHALLENGES, CATHOLIC SCRIPTURAL ANSWERS PART I

Chapter 6:

What Role Does the Bible Play?

A Catholic evangelist was giving a public talk on Tradition, which means the process by which the Church preserves and hands on divinely-revealed Truth. In our Catholic understanding, the Bible and Tradition are not opposed (as some Protestants believe); instead, the Bible is *part of* our sacred Tradition, but not the only part.

During the question-and-answer period after the talk, a polite but stubborn Bible Christian wanted to know what connection there could possibly be between God's Word in the Bible, and "this Tradition business," as he called it. The Catholic began his response by asking, "Do you have a Bible here?" "Yes," the Protestant answered as he handed it to the speaker. The Catholic frowned and said, "No, I mean a *Bible*, the Holy Scriptures, not that book of fairy tales you have there." The Protestant exclaimed in shock, "Fairy tales! What do you mean, 'fairy tales'? I'll have you know, sir, this is the Word of God, the Book of books!" The Catholic evangelist asked, "How do you know this book is God's Word; how do you know it's divine? It could be merely a book of fables collected by some smart people in the old days." "It's nothing of the sort!" the Protestant insisted. "I *know* it's the Word of God; my father told me so, just as my grandfather told him, and my great-grandfather told him." The Catholic smiled and said, "*That's* what we Catholics mean by Tradition, and that's why it goes hand-in-hand with the Bible. God's Word has been handed down to us—and God used the Catholic Church to do this."

According to the *Catechism of the Catholic Church,* "the Church has always venerated the Scriptures as she venerates the Lord's Body. She never ceases to present to the faithful the bread of life, taken from the one table of God's Word and Christ's Body" (par. 103). Thus, there is an unbreakable unity between Scripture and the Eucharist (and also Scripture and the authority of the Church, which provides the Eucharist, and the other Sacraments, to God's people). The Church acknowledges and presents Sacred Scripture as the Word of God (par. 104)—but this Word must be fully recognized and properly understood:

> . . . the Christian faith is not a "religion of the book." Christianity is the religion of the "Word" of God, not a written and mute word, but incarnate and living. If the Scriptures are not to remain a dead letter, Christ, the eternal Word of the living God, must, through the Holy Spirit, "open [our] minds to understand the Scriptures" (par. 108).
>
> Thus, the Bible is part of a living or dynamic process of transmitting and interpreting God's Word; as the *Catechism* further states, according to a saying of [Church] Fathers, Sacred Scripture is written principally in the Church's heart rather than in documents and records, for the Church carries in her Tradition the living memorial of God's Word, and it is the Holy Spirit Who gives her the spiritual interpretation of the Scripture (par. 113).

In other words, we might say that Tradition means, in part, allowing the Holy Spirit to guide the Church to a deeper understanding of the meaning of the Bible, particularly in regard to what it has to say to Christians living in today's world. This important perspective—indeed, this profound openness to the fullness of the truth—is most fully present in Catholicism.

It is unfortunately true, that, following the Protestant Reformation, the Catholic Church became somewhat "defensive" about the use of the Bible—but that's not surprising, as many Protestants were trying to use Sacred Scripture as a "weapon" against the Church. As the folly of Martin Luther's willingness to let each believer interpret the Bible for him- or herself became apparent, Catholicism understandably reemphasized the importance of correctly interpreting Scripture—i.e., in a way consistent with the Church's ongoing Tradition, which stretches back to and includes the authors of the New Testament books themselves.

(By way of analogy, no knowledgeable American would take seriously the idea that each citizen can interpret the U. S. Constitution for him- or herself, without any reference to constitutional law, legal precedents, and the writings and intentions of the Founding Fathers; Americans acknowledge, moreover, the unique authority of the Supreme Court to have the final say on what the Constitution means and on how it's to be applied in particular legal cases. Seen in this light, Catholicism's insistence that the Church—which, unlike the Supreme Court, has Christ's promise of the ongoing presence and guidance of the Holy Spirit—has a unique authority to interpret Scripture is quite reasonable and legitimate.)

There were sometimes overreactions on the part of individual Catholic pastors and teachers (resulting in some of the laity gaining an impression that they should carefully limit their personal reading of Scripture, and that Bible study was something Catholics just didn't do), but these ideas and attitudes—which were never official Church practice—have long since disappeared. The Second Vatican Council (1962-65), for instance, used biblical images to help Catholics find their "roots," describing the Church as the People of God, the Body of Christ, the sheepfold, the vineyard of God, the temple of the Holy Spirit, and a pilgrim community. New translations of the Bible (e.g., *The Jerusalem Bible* and *The New American Bible*) were authorized, and the Lectionary (the book containing the Scripture readings used at Mass) was revised so as to use a three-year cycle of readings, thereby presenting Sunday Mass-goers with a much wider and richer selection of the Bible's treasures. (Interestingly, many Protestant congregations use a lectionary closely based on the Catholic version.)

Sacred Scripture plays a vital and essential role in the life of the Catholic Church; indeed, the Bible can rightly be called "the Catholic Church's Book," for it was the Church—under the guidance of the Holy Spirit—which wrote the New Testament, decided which Old Testament and other books would be included in the Bible as canonical, and which preserved the Scriptures as we now have them (something Luther himself acknowledged).

Nevertheless, this doesn't keep some Protestants from attempting to use the Bible against the Church, trying to "prove" that Catholic beliefs and practices are mistaken or unscriptural. They act as if the Bible can be separated from the Church (as if it suddenly dropped down from Heaven one day), seeming to believe it's self-validating and can easily and correctly be interpreted by individual believers, without any reference to the Church's magisterium (teaching authority). This idea is obviously incorrect, for since the Bible is the Church's Book, she alone is uniquely qualified to interpret it. Moreover, to every Protestant scriptural challenge, there's a compelling Catholic answer, based not only on Tradition, but on Scripture itself.

Chapter 7:

Sola Scriptura

Sola Scriptura (Latin for "Scripture alone") is one of the two central claims of Protestantism (the other being *Sola Fide*, which will be covered in the next chapter).

This Protestant belief says that only the Bible, and not any "man-made traditions" (the derogatory term some Protestants use for Tradition and the Church's magisterium) can serve as an authority on matters of Christian religious belief and practice. (In other words, if it isn't specifically mentioned and approved of in Scripture, it isn't valid.)

In response to this, Catholicism teaches that Scripture (as noted in the previous chapter) is indeed an essential and irreplaceable means of transmitting God's Word; however, Tradition also plays a vital role in this process. Jesus promised His followers that the Holy Spirit would always be present and active in the Church, and so in a certain sense, God's revelation doesn't end with the writing of the New Testament; the Holy Spirit continues to guide the Church in matters of faith and morals. (*Formal Revelation* is complete in the person of Jesus Christ; however, as the *Catechism* states, "Yet even if Revelation is already complete, it has not been made completely explicit; it remains for Christian faith gradually to grasp its full significance over the course of the centuries" — par. 66.)

It was the Catholic Church that, guided by the Holy Spirit, determined which writings would be in the Bible — and because Protestant Bibles are almost the same as Catholic Bibles (lacking only seven Old Testament books), Protestants themselves rely upon the authority of the Church in choosing to accept certain books as scriptural. (The final form of the Bible as we know it was only decided upon at the Council of Hippo in 393.) As one former Protestant wrote, "I realized that by looking to the Church as an authentic and reliable Witness to the canon, I was violating the principle of *sola Scriptura*. The 'Bible only' theory turned out to be self-refuting, since it cannot tell us which books belong in it and which don't!"[1]

If it weren't for the Catholic Church, the Bible — especially the New Testament — would not exist, and no other Christians would have access to it; for this reason, the Catholic Church is uniquely qualified to discern, interpret, and teach the true meaning of Scripture.

(In the examination of Scripture presented here and in chapters 8 - 15, all the passages are taken from the *New International Version,* a leading *Protestant* translation of the Bible.)

Scriptural Proofs of the Catholic Teaching:

Mt. 16:19 - "I [Jesus] will give you [Peter] the keys to the kingdom of Heaven; whatever you bind on earth will be bound in Heaven, and whatever you loose on earth will be loosed in Heaven." ***Comment:*** St. Peter and his successors (the Popes) have authority from Christ to interpret and define what the Bible says and what it means to be a Christian.

Lk. 10:16 - "He who listens to you [the apostles] listens to Me; he who rejects you rejects Me; but he who rejects Me rejects Him Who sent Me."
Comment: Accepting and living by the teachings and traditions of the Church brings us into direct contact with Christ Himself, but knowingly rejecting the authority of the Church makes it impossible for us to be true disciples of Christ.

Jn. 14:16 - "And I will ask the Father, and He will give you another Counselor [the Holy Spirit] to be with you forever—the Spirit of truth."
Comment: Jesus promised that His Church would always be guided by the Holy Spirit—not only until the Bible was compiled in its final form (393), but until the end of time.

Jn. 14:25-26 - "All this I have spoken to you while still with you. But the Counselor, the Holy Spirit, Whom the Father will send in My Name, will teach you all things and will remind you of everything I have said to you."
Comment: Because of the Holy Spirit, the Church's teachings are authentic and true to the teachings of Christ Himself.

1 Th. 2:13 - "And we also thank God continually because, when you received the word of God, *which you heard from us* [emphasis added], you accepted it not as the word of men, but as it actually is, the word of God, at work in you who believe."
Comment: Paul's letters to the Thessalonians (which most scholars agree were written about 49-50, making them the earliest New Testament

writings) came *after* the oral sharing of the Church's teachings and traditions.

Jn. 20:30 - "Jesus did many other miraculous signs in the presence of His disciples, *which are not recorded in this book*" [emphasis added].
Comment: The apostles were aware of many things which were not written down—teachings, sayings, and reflections which became part of the Church's Tradition.

Eph. 3:10-11 - "His [God's] intent was that now, *through the church* [emphasis added], the manifold wisdom of God should be made known to the rulers and heavenly realms, according to His eternal purpose which He accomplished in Christ Jesus our Lord." **Comment:** It was *through the Church* that God intended for the message of salvation to be made known.

There are many other passages emphasizing or supporting the Church's teaching authority, including Mt. 18:17-18; Mt. 28:19-20; Jn. 16:13-14; Acts 15; 1 Cor. 11:2; 2 Th. 3:16; Eph. 3:4-6, 10-11; Col. 1:18; 1 Tim. 3:15; 2 Tim. 2:2; Heb. 13:7-8; 1 Pt. 1:20-21; 2 Pt. 1:20; 2 Pt. 3:16.

Nowhere does the Bible itself say that Scripture alone is the source of God's truth (thus making the Protestant belief in *sola Scriptura* a "man-made tradition"). The best defense of this mistaken belief Protestants can present is 2 Tim. 3:16 ("All Scripture is God-breathed and is useful for teaching, rebuking, correcting and training in righteousness"), but this passage doesn't say that *only* Scripture is valid for this purpose. Therefore, if ever a Protestant challenges a Catholic to "Show me where *that's* in the Bible," a valid response is, "First show me where the Bible says that every Church teaching has to *be* in the Bible."

Chapter 8:

Sola Fide

Besides *sola Scriptura, sola fide* ("by faith alone") is the other major foundational belief of Protestantism. Martin Luther was convinced the Catholic Church overemphasized good deeds at the expense of faith (and in fact, some individual Catholics were guilty of this mistake). Luther, however, went to the opposite extreme and denied that good works have any role whatsoever in the process of salvation, and—in terms of being saved—are unnecessary and even useless.

The Catholic teaching presents a much more balanced understanding; the Church teaches that while only faith in Jesus Christ can save us, it must be a *living faith*—in other words, one demonstrated by our moral decisions and our actions in daily life. We certainly can't "earn" our salvation, because salvation is a free gift from God—but once we accept this gift, it must make a difference in how we live. (In fairness to present-day Lutheranism, it should be noted that Catholic and Lutheran leaders and scholar have issue some joint statements on justification which demonstrate substantial agreement on this issue—but this doesn't eliminate the need for Catholics to understand the Church's teaching.)

We might say that faith and good deeds are two sides of the same coin—with faith coming before the good deeds. The two can't be separated, as Luther tried to do. (It's interesting and instructive that the only place the expression "by faith alone," or *sola fide*, appears in the Bible is James 2:24, which says that "we are *not* justified [saved] by faith alone"—thereby contradicting and invalidating Luther's position.

Scriptural Proofs of the Catholic Teaching:

Mt. 7:21 - "Not everyone who says to Me, 'Lord, Lord,' will enter the kingdom of Heaven, but only he who *does the will* of My Father Who is in Heaven."
Comment: Knowing Jesus isn't enough; we must also *live by* His teachings and commandments.

Mt. 19:16-21 - (When a rich young man asked Jesus what he had to do to gain eternal life, Jesus told him to *obey the commandments*.)

Comment: Good deeds, in the form of obedience to the commandments, are necessary to enter Heaven.

Mt. 25:31-46 - (In the parable of the sheep the goats, Jesus states that we will be judged on *what we do, or fail to do, for others.*)
Comment: Noting in this passage suggests that merely believing in Jesus is enough to merit salvation.

Jas. 1:22 - "Do not merely listen to the word, and so deceive yourselves. Do what it says."
Comment: They are deceived who consider it unnecessary to act upon what they believe.

Jas. 2:14,17-24 - "What good is it, my brothers, if a man claims to have faith but has no deeds? Can such faith save him? . . . Faith by itself, if it is not accompanied by action, is dead. But someone will say, 'You have faith; I have deeds.' Show me your faith without deeds, and I will show you my faith by what I do. You believe that there is one God. Good! Even the demons believe that—and shudder. You foolish man, do you want evidence that faith without deeds is useless? Was not our ancestor Abraham considered righteous for what he did when he offered his son Isaac on the altar? You see that his faith and his actions were working together, and his faith was made complete by what he did. And the scripture was fulfilled that says, 'Abraham believed God, and it was credited to him as righteousness,' and he was called God's friend. You see that a person is justified by what he does and not by faith alone."
Comment: This passage very clearly illustrates the deficiency of the *sola fide* theory.

Phil. 2:12 - "Therefore, my dear friends, as you have always obeyed— not only in my presence, but now much more in my absence—continue to *work out your salvation* [emphasis added] with fear and trembling. . . ."
Comment: St. Paul doesn't regard salvation as a gift we passively accept from God, but as something calling for our active cooperation.

1 Jn. 3:18-19 - "Dear children, let us not love with words or tongue *but with actions* [emphasis added] and in truth. This then is how we know that we belong to the truth. . . ."

Comment: Genuine love—which shows our acceptance of the gift of salvation—must be demonstrated in action.

Other passages supporting the Catholic teaching include Mt. 6:3-6; Mt. 7:20; Jn. 3:20; Jn. 14:21; Jn. 15:14; Acts 10:34-35; Acts 13:43; Rom. 2:6, 13; 1 Cor. 1:18; Gal. 5;6; Gal. 6:7-10; 1 Tim. 4:16; 1 Jn. 2:4; 1 Jn. 5:2-4.

Rm. 3:28 says, "For we maintain that a man is justified by faith apart from observing the law" (meaning the Law of Moses). When Luther translated the Letter to the Romans into German, he deliberately inserted the word "alone" after the phrase "justified by faith" so as to make this verse say what he wanted it to say.

When later criticized for this offense against God's Word—an offense Scripture itself specifically forbids (cf. Rv. 22:19)—he responded, "If your Papist [Catholic] makes such an unnecessary row about the word 'alone,' say right out to him: 'Dr. Martin Luther will have it so,' and say: 'Papists and asses are one and the same thing.' I will have it so, and I order it to be so, and my will is reason enough. I know very well the word 'alone' is not in the Latin or the Greek text, and it was not necessary for the Papists to tell me that. It is true those letters are not in it, which letters the jackasses look at, as a cow stares at a new gate. . . . It shall remain in my New Testament, and if all the Popish donkeys were to get mad and besides themselves, they will not get it out."[1]

Needless to say, Luther's defense of his position—besides being decidedly non-ecumenical—is anything but scriptural, and the weakness of his position demonstrates that *sola fide*—like *sola Scriptura*—is merely a "man-made tradition."

Chapter 9:

The Eucharist

As Catholics, we believe the Eucharist (Holy Communion) is *truly* and completely the Body and Blood of Christ—but many Protestants do not accept this. Some denominations see it as merely symbolic; others believe that in some degree the Eucharist is Christ's Body and Blood, but that it also continues to be bread and wine, or that it's the Eucharist only for a certain length of time (i.e., only until the end of their communion service), or that the bread and wine become Eucharist not through any sacramental action, but solely through the faith of the gathered community.

Protestants also reject the idea of the Eucharist as a sacrifice, insisting that Christ's perfect Sacrifice cannot be repeated. However, the Catholic Church doesn't claim to *repeat* it; rather, each time we celebrate Mass, His one, perfect Sacrifice is *made present* once again. Because of Christ's human nature, His Eucharistic action occurred at a certain time and place (in Jerusalem at the house of the Last Supper on Holy Thursday). Because of Christ's divine nature, however, this action rises above the limitations of time and space and takes on an eternal significance and presence. This means that each time we celebrate Mass (with a validly ordained priest presiding), we break free of the limits of time and space and "tap into" the reality of this one eternal Sacrifice.

Jesus would not have told the apostles "Do this in memory of Me" (Lk. 22:19) without giving them (and the Church) the power and authority to continue changing bread and wine into His Body and Blood. As the *Catechism* teaches,

> In order to leave them a pledge of [His] love, in order never to depart from His own and to make them sharers in His Passover, [Jesus] instituted the Eucharist as the memorial of His death and Resurrection, and commanded the apostles to celebrate it until His return; thereby He constituted them priests of the New Testament (par.1337).

To deny the Real Presence of Jesus in the Eucharist is to place limitations on His Divine power and on His love for His people—and this is something His Church will never do.

Scriptural Proofs of the Catholic Teaching:

Jn. 6:53-58 - "Jesus said to them [the Jews], 'I tell you the truth, unless you eat the flesh of the Son of Man and drink His blood, you have no life in you. Whoever eats My flesh and drinks My blood has eternal life, and I will raise him up at the last day. For My flesh is real food and My blood is real drink. Whoever eats My flesh and drinks My blood remains in Me, and I in him. Just as the living Father sent Me and I live because of the Father, so the one who feeds on Me will live because of Me. This is the bread that came down from Heaven. Your forefathers ate manna and died, but he who feds on this bread will live forever.'"

Comment: Jesus speaks very clearly of the need to eat His Body and drink His blood—not in a symbolic way, but in an actual one.

Jn. 6:60:66 - "On hearing it [Jesus' teaching on the Eucharist given in the previous passage], many of His disciples said, 'This is a hard teaching. Who can accept it? . . . From this time many of His disciples turned back and no longer followed Him."

Comment: If Jesus had been speaking only in symbolic terms, people would not have found this to be a "hard teaching." Moreover, when His disciples walked away, Jesus didn't call out, "Wait! You misunderstood Me," and instead of compromising on His teaching, He was even willing to risk losing the apostles (6:67).

Lk. 22:19-20 - "And He took bread, gave thanks and broke it, and gave it to them, saying, 'This is My Body given for you; do this in remembrance of Me.' In the same way, after the supper He took the cup, saying, 'This cup is the new covenant in My Blood, which is poured out for you."

Comment: At the Last Supper Jesus gave His Body and Blood to the apostles; He didn't say, "This is a symbol of My Body," but said, "This *is* My Body." He also gave the Church authority to repeat this Sacrament ("*Do this* in remembrance of Me").

1 Cor. 10:16 - "Is not the cup of thanksgiving for which we give thanks a participation in the Blood of Christ? And is not the bread that we break a participation in the Body of Christ?"

Comment: Through the Eucharist (a term which comes from the Greek word for *thanksgiving*), we share in the actual Body and Blood of

Christ—just as the apostles did at the Last Supper.

1 Cor. 11:23-26 - "For *I received from the Lord* [emphasis added] what I also passed on to you: The Lord Jesus, on the night He was betrayed, took bread, and when He had given thanks, He broke it and said, 'This is My Body, which is for you; do this in remembrance of Me.' In the same way, after supper He took the cup, saying, 'This cup is the new covenant in My Blood; do this, whenever you drink it, in remembrance of Me.' For whenever you eat this bread and drink this cup, you proclaim the Lord's death until He comes."

Comment: St. Paul claims his understanding of the Eucharist came from the Lord: namely, the Body and Blood of Christ *are truly given* under the appearance of bread and wine.

1 Cor. 11:27-31 - "Therefore, whoever eats the break or drinks the cup of the Lord in an unworthy manner will be guilty of sinning against the Body and Blood of the Lord. A man ought to examine himself before he eats of the bread and drinks of the cup. For anyone who eats and drinks without recognizing the Body of the Lord eats and drinks judgment on himself. That is why many among you are sick, and a number of you have fallen asleep. But if we judged ourselves, we would not come under judgment."

Comment: If the Eucharist were merely symbolic, Paul wouldn't have been so concerned over the possibility of Christians receiving it unworthily (that is, in a state of sin).

In addition to these scriptural passages, writings of the early Church Fathers also testify to belief in the "Real Presence" of Christ in the Eucharist. For instance, St. Ignatius of Antioch, writing no more than ten to fifteen years after the death of the last apostle, St. John, told the Christians in Ephesus that they were "to obey [the] bishop and clergy with undivided minds and to share in the common breaking of the bread—the medicine of immortality and the sovereign remedy by which we escape death and live in Jesus Christ forevermore" (Epistle to the Ephesians, 20:3).

Ignatius also wrote, "The sole Eucharist you should consider valid is one that is celebrated by the bishop himself or by some person authorized by him [that is, a validly ordained priest]. Where the bishop is to be seen, there let all the people be, just as wherever Jesus Christ is present, there is the Catholic Church" (Epistle to the Smyrmaeans, 8:1-2).

The *earliest* traditions of Christianity insist upon the Real Presence of Christ in the Eucharist—a belief that has always been preserved in Catholic doctrine and practice. Protestant claims that the Eucharist is only symbolic only arose 1500 years later, and are once again merely a "man-made tradition."

Chapter 10:

Church Structure and Authority

Because of their belief in *sola Scriptura* (the idea that the Bible is the only authority Christians need to recognize), many Protestants deny the need for an organized Church structure or hierarchy, and for a teaching authority or magisterium. Martin Luther's concept of the "priesthood of all believers" meant that each person can interpret the Bible for him- or herself, instead of relying on the teachings and authority of religious leaders.

This idea of individual interpretation of Scripture may sound plausible, but in practice it has proven disastrous. Luther revolted against the God-given authority of the Catholic Church, and many people followed him into revolt—but later some of them in turn rebelled against the authority of Luther and the other Reformers (and once Luther had established the precedent of rebelling against Church authority, he had no basis for opposing those who rejected his authority and leadership).

When each believer can personally decide the meaning of Scripture and Christian teaching, it's impossible to maintain any lasting religious unity—for whenever there's a disagreement (and because of our sinful human nature, there will *always* be some misunderstandings, hurt feelings, or disputes), people will break away and form a new congregation or denomination more to their liking . . . over and over again. That's why there are now over *27,000* different Protestant denominations—and this is certainly in opposition to Christ's will, for at the Last Supper He prayed that all His followers would be one (Jn. 17:21). In the words of one former Protestant (who himself struggled with this issue before converting to Catholicism), "How could Protestantism be [Christ's] 'church' when Protestant was nothing but disintegration, splintered, not unified, a frightening proliferation of squabbling, competing de-nominations, many masquerading under the title 'non-denominational?'"[1]

Only the Catholic Church can claim to have preserved the unity, and authority, Jesus desires. Some Protestants—especially those in non-denominational churches—claim that only a "spiritual" church is necessary (meaning a loose fellowship of believers), but of more than 100 New Testament references to "church," not one speaks of it in a merely spiritual sense. Scripture instead supports the Catholic understanding of the Church as a visible, identifiable (or structured) sign of Christ's presence and source of His truth and grace.

Scriptural Proofs of the Catholic Teaching:

Mt. 16:18-19 - "And I tell you that you are Peter, and on this rock I will build My Church, and the gates of Hades [Hell] will not overcome it. I will give you the keys of the kingdom of Heaven; whatever you bind on earth will be bound in Heaven, and whatever you loose on earth will be loosed in Heaven."

Comment: In appointing Peter as the head of the Church, Jesus gave him and his successors full authority, and promised that the Church would be spiritually triumphant over evil. Some persons will attempt to claim that the "rock" mentioned by Jesus isn't Peter personally, but a vague attitude of faith on the part of all true believers. This idea, however, has long since been discredited by serious Catholic *and* Protestant biblical scholars; there's overwhelming scholarly agreement that Peter alone is the rock to which Jesus refers.

Lk. 22:31-32 - "Simon [Peter], Simon, Satan has asked to sift you like wheat. But I have prayed for you, Simon, that your faith may not fail. And when you have turned back, strengthen your brothers."

Comment: Peter's ministry is to strengthen other members of the Church (and this implies that other Christians *need* this service). Because of Jesus' prayer, Peter's ministry is rooted in strength, for as Jas. 5:16 says, "The prayer of a righteous man is powerful and effective"—and there is no one more righteous than Jesus.

Jn. 21:15-17 - (Three times Jesus asked Peter, "Do you love Me?," and then told him, "Feed My sheep.")
Comment: Jesus entrusted His Church to the leadership and ministry of Peter.

Col. 1:18 - "And He [Jesus] is the head of the body, the church; He is the beginning and the firstborn from the dead, so that in everything He might have the supremacy."

Comment: Jesus is the head of the Church, and has full authority over her—including the authority to entrust her to the leadership of the apostles and their successors.

1 Cor. 12:28 - "And in the church God has appointed first of all apostles, second prophets, third teachers, then workers of miracles, also those having gifts of healing, those able to help others, those with gifts of administration, and those speaking in different kinds of tongues."

Comment: God Himself established a hierarchy, or order, within the Church.

Acts 2:42 - "They devoted themselves to the apostles' teaching and to the fellowship, to the breaking of bread and to prayer."

Comment: The earliest Christians made themselves subject to the apostles' authority and leadership in all religious and spiritual matters.

Acts 15:28 - "It seemed good to the Holy Spirit *and to us* [emphasis added] not to burden you with anything. . . ."

Comment: In deciding that pagan converts to Christianity need not first be circumcised according to the Law of Moses, the leaders of the Church directly identified their authority with that of the Holy Spirit.

1 Tim. 3:15 - "The church of the living God [is] the *pillar and foundation* [emphasis added] of the truth."

Comment: The Church is clearly identified as the custodian of the truths necessary for salvation.

Jude 3 - "Dear friends, although I was very eager to write to you about the salvation we share, I felt I had to write and urge you to contend for the faith that *was once entrusted to the saints*" [emphasis added].

Comment: The message of salvation has been entrusted to the saints (i.e., the Church) *once for all* (and thus, the Church's structure helps preserve this message).

Other scriptural passages supporting the Catholic teaching on the structure and authority of the Church include Acts 20:28; Eph.1:22-23; Eph. 2: 19-21; Eph. 5:30; Titus 1:5; 1 Tim. 5:17; Heb. 13:7-8, and 1 Pt. 5:1.

In addition to these many scriptural references, the historical validity of a hierarchical Church structure is also attested to in early Christian writings. For instance, St. Clement of Rome, writing before the end of the 1st century, said, "The apostles received the Gospel for us from the Lord Jesus Christ; and Jesus Christ was sent from God. Christ, therefore, is from God, and the apostles from Christ. Both of these orderly arrangements, then, are God's will. Receiving their instructions and being full of confidence on account of the resurrection of our Lord Jesus Christ, and confirmed in faith by the Word of God, they went forth in complete assurance of the Holy Spirit, preaching the Good News that the kingdom of God is coming. Through countryside and city they preached; and they appointed their earliest converts, testing them by the spirit, to be the bishops and deacons of future believers. Nor was this a novelty: for bishops and deacons had been written about a long time earlier. Indeed, Scripture somewhere says: 'I will set up their bishops in righteousness and their deacons in faith'" (Epistle to the Corinthians, 42:1-5).

SECTION C:

PROTESTANT CHALLENGES, CATHOLIC SCRIPTURAL ANSWERS PART II

Chapter 11:

Authority to Forgive Sins

Following the lead of Martin Luther, Protestants often deny that Penance or Reconciliation is a Sacrament, and they reject the idea that the Church has authority to forgive sins in Christ's Name (for this, they think, would detract from Christ's unique role as Savior). Any sins committed after Baptism can be forgiven, they claim, without reference to the Church—simply by repenting and asking God's forgiveness; no Sacrament (other than Baptism) is needed to receive God's mercy.

In contrast, Catholicism teaches that Penance or Reconciliation *is* one of the seven Sacraments instituted by Christ and entrusted to His Church. While it's true that we can and should privately pray for God's forgiveness as soon as we become conscious of having sinned, there are also times when this process of repentance and forgiveness is rightly experienced through the direct ministry of the Church.

As the *Catechism* explains, "Sin is before all else an offense against God, a rupture of communion with Him. At the same time it damages communion with the Church. For this reason conversion entails both God's forgiveness and reconciliation with the Church, which are expressed and accomplished liturgically by the Sacrament of Penance and Reconciliation" (par. 1440).

Baptism frees us from original sin (and also cleanses us of any personal sins we may have committed before we were baptized), but Christians can, and unfortunately, do, return to their sinful ways, thus needing to be reconciled with Christ and His Body, the Church. Jesus established the Sacrament of Penance because He foresaw this need. (Since Baptism cannot be repeated, it would have been shortsighted of Him not to make some provision for forgiving baptized sinners.)

To claim Christ didn't give the Church power to forgive sinners not only denies His knowledge of human nature (and Jn. 2:25 states that He was fully aware of everything in the human heart); it also places limits on His mercy—something no one has the right to do.

Scriptural Proofs of the Catholic Teaching:

Mt. 16:18-19 - "And I tell you that you are Peter, and on this rock I will build My Church, and the gates of Hades [Hell] will not overcome it. I will give you the keys of the kingdom of Heaven; whatever you bind on earth will be bound in Heaven, and *whatever you loose on earth will be loosed in Heaven*" [emphasis added].

Comment: Jesus gave Peter authority to "bind and loose," which includes the right to forgive sins in His Name. (To forgive and save sinners, after all, was Christ's foremost concern and the reason He came to earth—so it's only natural He would involve Peter and his successors in this same ministry.)

Jn. 2:23-25 - "Now while He was in Jerusalem at the Passover Feast, many people saw the miraculous signs He was doing and believed in His name. But Jesus would not entrust Himself to them, for He knew all men. He did not need man's testimony about man, for He knew what was in a man."

Comment: Jesus was an expert on human nature; as such, He completely understood the realities of sin and guilt, and recognized the ongoing need for sinners to be reconciled. Like the man who built his house solidly on rock (cf. Mt. 7:24-25), He created a solid foundation for His Church by giving her authority to forgive sins.

Jn. 20:21-23 - "Again Jesus said, 'Peace be with you! As the Father has sent Me, I am sending you.' And with that He breathed on them and said, 'Receive the Holy Spirit. If you forgive anyone his sins, they are forgiven; if you do not forgive them, they are not forgiven.'"

Comment: On Easter Sunday Jesus gave all the apostles the authority to forgive sins in His Name and through the power of the Holy Spirit—and because the Spirit is always with the Church (cf. Jn. 14:16), the successors of the apostles also have this authority.

Mt. 6:14-15 - "For if you forgive men when they sin against you, your heavenly Father will also forgive you. But if you do not forgive men their sins, your Father will not forgive your sins."

Comment: *All Christians* must forgive sinners, and doing so (or failing to do so) will be the basis for God's own judgment. If Jesus gives this authority and responsibility to individual believers, it is logically given in an even greater and more important way to the Church which His followers comprise.

Mt. 18:15-18 - "If your brother sins against you, go and show him his fault, just between the two of you. If he listens to you, you have won your brother over. But if he will not listen, take one or two others along, so that every matter may be established by the testimony of two witnesses. If he refuses to listen to them, tell it to the church; and if he refuses to listen even to the church, treat him as you would a pagan or a tax collector."

Comment: Jesus here presents the Church as the final arbiter of right and wrong, and as the ultimate source of the forgiveness of sins in His Name (so much so that Christians are to shun those who reject the Church's authority).

2 Cor. 2:10 - "If you forgive anyone, I also forgive him. And what I have forgiven—if there was anything to forgive—*I have forgiven in the sight of Christ* [emphasis added] for your sake. . . ."

Comment: St. Paul here refers to the concept of forgiving others in the Name of Christ.

2 Cor. 5:18-20 - "All this is from God, Who reconciled us to Himself through Christ and *gave us the ministry of reconciliation* [emphasis added]: that God was reconciling the world to Himself in Christ, not counting men's sins against them. And *He has committed to us the message of reconciliation* [emphasis added]. We are therefore Christ's ambassadors, as though God Himself were making His appeal through us. We implore you on Christ's behalf: Be reconciled to God."

Comment: According to St. Paul, God has given the Church the ministry of reconciliation.

Jas. 5:14-16 - "Is any one of you sick? He should call the elders of the church to pray over him and to anoint him with oil in the name of the

Lord. And the prayer offered in faith will make the sick person well; the Lord will raise him up. If he has sinned, he will be forgiven. Therefore *confess your sins to each other* [emphasis added] and pray for each other so that you may be healed. The prayer of a righteous man is powerful and effective."

    Comment: Even though God alone can forgive sins, St. James tells Christians to seek God's forgiveness by confessing their sins to others in the community—specifically, to the elders (designated leaders, or priests) mentioned in verse 14.

    Jas. 5:19-20 - "My brothers, if one of you should wander from the truth and someone should bring him back, remember this: Whoever turns a sinner from the error of his way will save him from death and cover a multitude of sins."

    Comment: Helping sinners repent is a great deed in God's eyes; thus, it's reasonable to believe that Christ would make this ministry of reconciliation an important part of the Church's mission.

    These passages make it very clear that Jesus entrusted His ministry of reconciliation to His Church. Therefore, the Catholic claim that Penance, or Reconciliation, is a Sacrament instituted by Christ has a solid scriptural foundation.

Chapter 12:

Being "Born Again"

Many Protestants—particularly Evangelicals and Pentecostalists—engage in missionary activity by directly asking people, "Have you been saved?," or "Have you been born again?" (This refers to Jn. 3:5, in which Jesus says, "No one can enter the kingdom of God unless he is born of water and the Spirit.")

Sometimes a simple answer will suffice, such as "Yes, I have, but thank you for asking," or "Yes, I have accepted Jesus Christ as my Lord and Savior." However, some evangelizers will continue to press the point, especially if they discover that one is a Catholic—for they frequently consider it their personal duty to "enlighten" Catholics and to rescue them from spiritual "slavery" in what they consider a false church. Therefore, Catholics should know what the Church teaches on the topic of salvation.

Salvation is a free gift from God, offered to us through His Son Jesus Christ, and made available to us through His Church—specifically through the Sacrament of Baptism. As the *Catechism* explains, "Through Baptism we are freed from sin and reborn as sons of God; we become members of Christ, are incorporated into the Church and made sharers in her mission" (par. 1213).

Being baptized with water in the Name of the Holy Trinity (cf. Mt. 28: 19) allows us to share in the saving death and resurrection of the Lord (cf. Rm. 6:4-5). However, contrary to what some Protestants suggest, this is not a once-and-for-all event (an idea sometimes expressed with the complacent or even smug assertion that once you've been saved, you cannot lose your salvation). Rather, salvation is an ongoing process which requires our active and continuing cooperation with God's grace.

We have already been "born again" in Baptism (which for most of us occurred when we were infants). If we later turn away from God through serious sin, but then repent, we don't have to be "born again"; we simply need to seek God's forgiveness (especially through the Sacrament of Reconciliation) and begin using His grace to live up to our Christian responsibilities.

Scriptural Proofs of the Catholic Teaching:

Rm. 6:4 - "We were therefore buried with Him [Christ Jesus] through baptism into death in order that, just as Christ was raised from the dead through the glory of the Father, we too may live a new life."

Comment: Baptism gives us a share in Christ's saving death and resurrection, and one who has been baptized does not later need to be "born again."

1 Cor. 9:27 - "I beat my body and make it my slave so that after I have preached to others, I myself will not be disqualified for the prize."

Comment: Even someone as holy and committed to Christ as St. Paul was aware of the possibility of losing his share in eternal life (and he remained firmly rooted in prayer, and engaged in constant fasts and other forms of penance, to guard against such a possibility).

Phil. 2:12-13 - *"Continue to work out your salvation* [emphasis added] with fear and trembling, for it is God Who works in you to will and to act according to His good purpose."

Comment: Paul indicates that salvation is an ongoing process which must be taken very seriously.

Phil. 3:10-12 - "I want to know Christ and the power of His resurrection and the fellowship of sharing in His sufferings, becoming like Him in His death, and so, somehow, to attain to the resurrection from the dead. Not that I have already obtained all this, or have already been made perfect, but I press on to take hold of that for which Christ Jesus took hold of me."

Comment: In this passage Paul does not consider that he has already obtained salvation; his ongoing and active cooperation with God's grace is necessary.

Mt. 7:21-24 - "Not everyone who says to Me, 'Lord, Lord,' will enter the kingdom of heaven, but only he who does the will of My Father Who is in heaven. Many will say to Me on that day, 'Lord, Lord, did we not prophesy in Your Name, and in Your Name drive out demons and perform many miracles?' Then I will tell them plainly, 'I never knew you. Away from Me, you evildoers!' Therefore, everyone who hears these words of

Mine and puts them into practice is like a wise man who built his house on the rock."

Comment: Salvation can be lost even by persons who minister in Christ's Name—so we must continually strive to be faithful to Him.

Rm. 2:6-7 - "God will give to each person according to what He has done. To those who by *persistence* [emphasis added] in doing good seek glory, honor, and immortality, He will give eternal life."

Comment: We must persevere in using God's grace and in doing good if we are to reach Heaven.

Eph. 4:27 - "Do not give the devil a foothold."

Comment: This advice would be unnecessary if Christians had already achieved their salvation while here on earth; Satan's temptations are dangerous precisely because it's always possible for us to reject God's love.

2 Tim. 4:9-10 - "Do your best to come to me quickly, for Demas, because he loved this world, has deserted me."

Comment: Demas was once a missionary companion of Paul (see Col. 4:14 and Phlm 24), but he abandoned his calling from God.

1 Jn. 2:19 - "They [many antichrists] went out from us [the Church], but they did not really belong to us."

Comment: Even being a member of the Church does not guarantee salvation or perseverance in the Faith.

Catholic evangelist Steve Wood, a convert from Protestantism, wrote, "My chief opposition to Catholicism [when I was a Protestant] stemmed from my belief that the Catholic Church was leading millions of people to hell because of its teachings on salvation. I thought, as I had been told by countless Protestants . . . , that the Catholic Church denied that salvation was by grace alone. Since the Bible is clear that salvation is by grace, not by works, and since I thought the Catholic Church taught salvation by works, as far as I was concerned, Catholicism was fatally wrong. What I didn't realize was that the Catholic Church has consistently condemned the idea of salvation by works, teaching that salvation comes solely by God's free gift of grace. Later, when the Catholic position was explained to me, I was amazed at how often it is misrepresented and caricatured by Protestant critics."[1]

The Church's teaching on salvation is very simple and quite scriptural: Salvation is God's free gift, which the Church offers to us in the Sacrament of Baptism in obedience to Christ's command (cf. Mt. 28:19). Through Baptism, we are born again of water and the Holy Spirit (cf. Jn. 3:5), thereby sharing in Christ's death and resurrection (cf. Rm. 6:3-14), and if we remain in His grace, we will one day enter His Kingdom.

Chapter 13:

Purgatory

The Catholic Church's teaching on the existence of Purgatory is rejected as unscriptural by most Protestants, who frequently point out that the term doesn't appear anywhere in the Bible. That's correct; it's also true that the term "Trinity" isn't to be found in Scripture, but all Protestants still believe in the concept it expresses: Three Divine Persons in One God. The word "Trinity" is merely a word invented by the Church to express this truth, and in a similar manner, the term "Purgatory" refers to the place or state of existence of those in need of additional spiritual purification, or cleansing of their sins, after death.

The most direct scriptural reference to Purgatory is 2 Mc. 12:43-46, which describes how the great Jewish leader Judas Maccabaeus "took up a collection among all his soldiers, amounting to two thousand silver drachmas, which he sent to Jerusalem to provide for an expiatory sacrifice. In doing this he acted in a very excellent and noble way, inasmuch as he had the resurrection of the dead in view; for if he were not expecting the fallen to rise again, it would have been useless and foolish to pray for them in death. But if he did this with a view to the splendid reward that awaits those who had gone to rest in godliness, it was a holy and pious thought. Thus he made atonement for the dead that they might be freed from this sin" (*New American Bible* translation).

If it is an "excellent and noble" thing to pray for the dead, this must refer to persons experiencing what Catholicism calls Purgatory—for those in Heaven do not need our prayers, and those in Hell are beyond the help of our prayers. It should be noted, however, that many Protestants reject this argument for the simple reason that they consider 2 Maccabees (and six other Old Testament books found in Catholic Bibles) as *apochryphal*—that is, not an authentic part of the Bible. Even so, it's possible to show from other biblical passages that the concept of Purgatory has a solid scriptural foundation.

Scriptural Proofs of the Catholic Teaching:

Rv. 21:27 - "Nothing impure will ever enter it [the new Jerusalem— God's heavenly kingdom], nor will anyone who does what is shameful or deceitful, but only those whose names are written in the Lamb's book of life."

Comment: Anyone touched by sin is unworthy and unable to enter into Heaven—and since this includes everyone except Jesus and the Virgin Mary, obviously there must be some way in which sinners can be cleansed so as to be allowed entry into Heaven (including those whose lives are not long enough to complete this process while on earth).

1 Cor. 6:9 - "Do you not know that the wicked will not inherit the Kingdom of God?"

Comment: Heaven is not guaranteed to everyone, but only to those who are made worthy of it.

Mt. 18:34 - (In the parable of the royal official who refused to forgive a small debt owed to him, even though his master at first forgave his much larger debt,) "his master turned him over to the jailers to be tortured, until he should *pay back all he owed*" [emphasis added].

Comment: Jesus is obviously speaking symbolically, for no one can earn money to repay a financial debt while in prison. In giving this lesson on the need to forgive others, Our Lord is also referring to Purgatory.

Lk. 12:58-59 - "As you are going with your adversary to the magistrate, try hard to be reconciled with him on the way, or he may drag you off to the judge, and the judge turn you over to the officer, and the officer throw you into prison. I tell you, you will not get out until you have paid the last penny."

Comment: Again, Jesus is speaking symbolically (for merely spending time in jail will not pay a financial debt). Trying to settle accounts while on the way to court here means making amends for our sins while still on earth before facing God's judgment (and the prison cannot refer to Hell, as no one ever leaves there).

1 Cor. 3:12-15 - "If any man builds on this foundation [Christ] using gold, silver, costly stones, wood, hay or straw, his work will be shown for what it is, because the Day [of judgment] will bring it to light. It will be revealed with fire, and the fire will test the quality of each man's work. If what he has built survives, he will receive his reward. If it is burned up, he will suffer loss; he himself will be saved, *but only as one escaping through* *the flame*" [emphasis added].

Comment: Purgatory is often described as a purifying fire—through which, if necessary, we enter Heaven.

Phil. 2:10 - "At the Name of Jesus every knee should bow, in Heaven and on earth and *under the earth*" [emphasis added].

Comment: "Under the earth" can be understood as a reference to Purgatory, whose inhabitants—unlike those of Hell, do give their allegiance to Jesus.

Jude 23 - "Snatch others from the fire and save them."

Comment: Only Christ can save people from the fires of Hell, but our prayers and sacrifices can help those who are suffering in Purgatory—even to the point of assisting their spiritual purification, allowing them to enter Heaven that much sooner.

Rev. 6:9-11 - "When he [the Lamb] opened the fifth seal, I saw under the altar [in Heaven] the souls of those who had been slain because of the word of God and the testimony they had maintained. They called out in a loud voice, 'How long, Sovereign Lord, holy and true, until You judge the inhabitants of the earth and avenge our blood?' Then each of them was given a white robe, and they were told to *wait a little longer*" [emphasis added].

Comment: Even just persons may need to be purified of certain faults, such as a desire for revenge (which is contrary to Christ's teaching on forgiveness). That these persons are *under* the altar suggests that they have not yet achieved full membership in the Kingdom—indicating a process consistent with the Church's teaching on Purgatory.

The Church understands Purgatory as a final opportunity for sinners to satisfy the demands of Divine Justice—as humorously illustrated by an event which took place hundreds of years ago. When a cathedral was in need of repairs, the canons (priests assigned there) took the opportunity to add a small chapel dedicated to the souls in Purgatory. The artist hired to decorate it represented the suffering souls in the midst of the purifying flames—and included very prominently among them the abbot of a neighboring monastery. The abbot's likeness was unmistakable, and when he himself became aware of the situation, he complained to the canons, demanding that his image be removed. The artist refused, and the matter was brought before the archbishop.

When the archbishop asked the artist if he would alter his work by removing the abbot's image from the painting, he refused, giving this explanation: "Last year my lord the abbot stated in a sermon that those who die without having made satisfaction are detained in Purgatory until they have paid their debts. As it happens, his monastery still owes me 100 coins for work I did for them two years ago, and so I will not release him from my painting until this debt is paid." All in attendance, the abbot included, could not help but laugh at this explanation, and the abbot quickly made arrangements for the payment of the debt—leading the artist to modify his work, so that it showed the abbot as one being released from Purgatory and entering into God's presence in Heaven.[1]

It is true that we will not enter Heaven until we have paid the last penny of our debt to God (cf. Mt. 5:26)—and if this process isn't completed on earth, it must continue after death. As the *Catechism* teaches, "All who die in God's grace and friendship, but [are] still imperfectly purified, are indeed assured of their eternal salvation; but after death they undergo purification, so as to achieve the holiness necessary to enter the joy of Heaven" (par. 1030). All sins do spiritual harm to the sinner, and this harm must be completely healed before we can enter into the presence of the Lord. Our acts of love and faith, and our freely-chosen good deeds and sacrifices, can begin and perhaps even complete this process during our earthly lives, but if this experience of healing and purification is not complete by the time we die, God in His mercy allows us to continue it after death.

The Church also teaches that our prayers can assist those currently undergoing this cleansing process in Purgatory; St. John Chrysostom (d. 407) wrote, "Let us help and commemorate them [the dead]. If Job's sons were purified by their father's sacrifice [cf. Jb. 1:5], why would we doubt that our offerings for the dead bring them some consolation? Let us not hesitate to help those who have died and to offer our prayers for them."

Chapter 14:

Mary and the Saints

Virtually all Christians would agree that the Catholic Church is unique in the degree of honor it gives to Mary, the Mother of God. (Only the Orthodox Church accords her a similarly exalted status.) Indeed, it's not unknown for Protestants to accuse Catholics of "worshipping" Mary, while also objecting to the Catholic practice of praying to the saints and asking for their intercession. This, they assert, violates the First Commandment, in which God tells us we must worship no other gods but Him (Ex. 20:3). Moreover, "there is one God and one mediator between God and man, the man Jesus Christ" (1 Tim. 2:5). Therefore, Protestants claim, Catholics are wrong to treat any of the saints, particularly Mary, as another mediator between themselves and God.

The Church has always taught that God alone—Father, Son, and Holy Spirit—is worthy of our adoration and worship. Mary herself acknowledged that she was a mere creature, in need of a savior (Lk. 1:47). However, God freely chose Mary for the highest honor imaginable: to be the Mother of His Son. When *we* honor Mary, we are simply (though to a much lesser degree) following God's example. Moreover, if God wants us to honor our earthly mothers (cf. Ex. 20:12), surely He desires us to honor *His* Mother (and Mary can rightly be called the Mother of God because Jesus is truly divine, in addition to being truly human).

Mary certainly does not replace Jesus as our mediator with God; however, it pleases Christ to honor His Mother by giving her a share in His work of redemption. Jesus was subject to Mary during His earthly life (cf. Lk. 2:51), and she interceded with Him on behalf of those in need (cf. Jn. 2:3-5). If the prayer of a righteous person is very powerful (cf. Jas. 5:16), Mary's intercession for us is particularly effective, for she is "highly favored" in God's sight (Lk. 1:28). Indeed, the most common Catholic prayer in Mary's honor—the "Hail Mary"—is very scriptural, for it directly quotes the angel Gabriel's words to her (cf. Lk. 1:28ff), along with a request that she pray for us—which conforms to the scriptural command to intercede for each other (cf. 1 Tim. 2:1-4).

A similar explanation can be given for the honor Catholics give the other saints. There is no reason to believe Christians can no longer help and pray for their brothers and sisters on earth once they themselves are in Heaven. Indeed, because of the perfect love which exists in Heaven, the saints would presumably be even *more* willing and able to intercede for others than they were on earth. Praying to the saints is not the same as worshipping them; all the saints, except for Mary, were themselves sinners, and all the saints, including Mary, were themselves in need of God's free gift of salvation. By honoring the saints, we honor the God Who created them; we should ask for their prayers, just as we ask our fellow Christians on earth to pray for us.

Scriptural Proofs of the Catholic Teaching:

Gn. 3:15 - "And I [God] will put enmity between you [the serpent] and the woman, and between your offspring and hers; he will crush your head, and you will strike his heel."

Comment: The serpent, symbolizing Satan, tempted Eve and her husband Adam to disobey God's command, thereby introducing sin and death into the world. God thereupon announced His plan of salvation, in which a new Eve—Mary—would give birth to One Who would forever destroy Satan's power. (That Satan would cause severe harm to the Church through his temptations is suggested by a reference to striking at Christ's heel; this, however—unlike the crushing of the serpent's head—is not a decisive blow.) Mary, through her perfect obedience to the Lord (cf. Lk. 1:38), corrected or made up for Eve's act of disobedience.

Lk. 1:28 - "The angel went to her and said, 'Greetings, you who are highly favored! The Lord is with you."

Comment: Mary was highly favored in God's eyes (Lk. 1:30), and because of her perfect obedience, she remains in this state—which makes her, more than any other creature, worthy of our highest respect (though this is not, of course, equal to the worship we give to God). Because the Lord is with her, Mary is the perfect role model for us; by asking for her help and by imitating her example, we too can become pleasing to God.

Ps. 45:9,17 - "At your right hand is the royal bride in gold of Ophir. . . . I will perpetuate your memory through all generations; therefore the nations will praise you for ever and ever."

Comment: Mary is truly the Queen of Heaven (for Jesus was born of King David's royal line), and the Lord here states that she is to be praised by all nations throughout all ages.

Jn. 19:26-27 - "When Jesus saw His Mother there, and the disciple whom He loved standing nearby, He said to His Mother, 'Dear woman, here is your son,' and to the disciple, 'Here is your mother.'"

Comment: This disciple represents all Christians (for we are all loved by Christ); by giving us Mary to be our spiritual Mother, Jesus indicates His desire that we honor her. (Incidentally, this passage refutes the common Protestant claim, based on Mk. 6:3, that Jesus had earthly brothers and sisters. Not only was the term "brother" commonly used to include cousins and other blood or tribal relatives, but in 1st century Palestine it would have been unthinkable for a dying eldest son to entrust the care of his parents to someone outside the family if a sibling existed.)

Rv. 12:1-2 - "A great and wondrous sign appeared in heaven: a woman clothed with the sun, with the moon under her feet and a crown of twelve stars on her head. She was pregnant and cried out in pain as she was about to give birth."

Comment: Many scholars agree that the woman in this passage represents the Church; however, these verses are sometimes also interpreted as referring to Mary, for they tell us that her Son is destined to "rule all nations with an iron scepter" (v. 5). Christ's birth was indeed a great sign, and His Mother is shown as having an important role in redemption and in the struggle against evil. Satan wages war against her spiritual off-spring (v. 17); because Mary is a loving Mother, it makes sense for us to seek her help and protection in our own spiritual struggles in life.

1 Cor. 12:12-13,26-27 - "The body is a unit, though it is made up of many parts; and though all its parts are many, they form one body. So it is with Christ. For we were all baptized by one Spirit into one body— whether Jews or Greeks, slave or free—and we were all given the one Spirit to drink. . . . If one part suffers, every part suffers with it; if one part is honored, every part rejoices with it. Now you are the body of Christ, and each one of you is part of it."

Comment: Because of our unity as members of the Body of Christ, we must show concern for one another; this remains true even after we've entered the kingdom of Heaven.

Lk. 20:37-38 - "But in the account of the [burning] bush, even Moses showed that the dead rise, for he calls the Lord 'the God of Abraham, and the God of Isaac, and the God of Jacob.' He is not the God of the dead, but of the living, for to Him all are alive."

Comment: Jesus states that all are alive to God—and those who live in His presence can and must demonstrate love for others. The saints do this by interceding on our behalf in response to our prayers.

Eph. 3:14-18 - "For this reason I kneel before the Father, from whom *His whole family in heaven* [emphasis added] and on earth derives its name. I pray that out of His glorious riches He may strengthen you with power through His Spirit in your inner being, so that Christ may dwell in your hearts through faith. And I pray that you, being rooted and established in love, may have power, *together with all the saints* [emphasis added], to grasp how wide and long and high and deep is the love of Christ. . . ."

Comment: Through the love of God, believers in Christ are united both in Heaven and on earth.

1 Tim. 2:1,3 - "I urge, then, first of all, that requests, prayers, intercession and thanksgiving be made for everyone. . . . This is good, and pleases God our Savior. . . ."

Comment: If indeed it pleases God when we pray for others, the saints—who are perfect in love—surely must pray for us.

2 Cor. 1:10-11 - "On Him we have set our hope that He will continue to deliver us, as *you help us by your prayers* [emphasis added]. Then many will give thanks on our behalf for the gracious favor granted us *in answer to the prayers of many*" [emphasis added].

Comment: If a great saint like Paul could be helped by the prayers of imperfect Christians on earth, surely we can be helped even more by the prayers of those who are in Heaven after being made perfect through Christ's grace.

Catholics honor and esteem the saints—especially the Blessed Virgin Mary—but we do not worship them. Just as the moon has no light of its own, but merely reflects the light of the son, so Mary's radiance is derived from God, and it is through His grace that she achieved perfect holiness. One of the ways we praise God is by honoring Him for the beauty of

His creation (cf. Ps. 8, Ps. 104, Ps. 148)—and because Mary is the most perfect all of His creatures, it pleases God when we give her the highest possible honor.

Also, having paintings and statues of Mary and the other saints is no more idolatrous than keeping photographs of our loved ones; praying to them and asking their help is no more sinful than a widow or widower's practice of talking aloud to a deceased loved one at his or her gravesite. Referring to the saints, Heb. 12:1 states that "we are surrounded by such a great cloud of witnesses." The holy men and women of every age are—if we wish—intimately involved in our lives, and their witness or example can be a source of guidance and inspiration as we undergo our own struggles to be faithful to God. This truth is an important part of our Christian belief in the unity of the Body of Christ, a belief dating back to the earliest years of the Church—and Catholicism, more than any other religion, has preserved it. Let us "imitate those who through faith and patience inherit what has been promised" (Heb. 6:12).

Chapter 15:

Call No Man "Father"

A common challenge Catholics hear from Protestants is that by giving her priests the title "Father," the Church is violating Christ's command—for in Mt.23:9, Jesus says: "And do not call anyone on earth 'Father,' for you have one Father, and He is in Heaven." (Compared to the issues addressed in the preceding chapters, this is not a major theological point— but because it's a common objection of the Church's critics, it's worth exploring in some detail.)

Catholics interpret Mt. 23:9 as meaning that no one on earth may be given the honor due to God alone, for no human being is able to take God's place. In the context of this understanding, however, we are not literally forbidden to use the term "father" when appropriate (as is the case with our biological fathers).

God is truly our Father, yet He often chooses certain men to exercise this role on earth in (a vastly reduced and imperfect) imitation of His heavenly Fatherhood. For instance, in giving the Ten Commandments to Moses, God said, "Honor your *father* [emphasis added] and mother" (Ex. 20:12), clearly referring to our earthly parents. In the Book of Sirach (Ecclesiasticus) we read, "For the Lord sets a father in honor over his children" (3:2; *New American Bible* translation).

Catholics no more violate the spirit of Mt. 23:9 by referring to priests as "Father" than Protestants contradict Christ's teachings by referring to their ministers as "Pastor" or "Reverend." After all, *pastor* is the Latin word for "shepherd." In Jn. 10:11 Jesus calls Himself the "Good Shepherd" Who lays down His life for the sheep, in contrast to the hired hands who flee at the first sight of trouble. Does this means that Jesus is the *only* "good" shepherd or pastor, and that all others with this title are merely unfaithful hired hands? Of course not. The word "reverend" is defined as "worthy of reverence; venerable." However, in Mk. 10:18 Jesus says, "No one is good—except God alone." Does this make the use of the title "Reverend" blasphemous or a usurpation of God's goodness? Certainly not. Just as an earthly father gives his family name to his children, so God gives us the right to use certain titles and prerogatives (as long as we acknowledge His ultimate authority in all things).

Scriptural Proofs of the Catholic Teaching:

Lk. 16:24 - "So he [the rich man in Our Lord's parable] called up to him, 'Father Abraham, have pity on me and send Lazarus to dip the tip of his finger in water and cool my tongue, for I am in agony in this fire."
Comment: Jesus used the title "father" in reference to Abraham.

Acts 7:2 - "He [Stephen] replied, 'Brothers and fathers, listen to me!'"
Comment: When Stephen was on trial before the Sanhedrin (the Jewish Council in Jerusalem), he used the title "fathers" in reference to the religious elders.

Acts 22:1 - [Paul said:] "Brothers and fathers, listen now to my defense."
Comment: St. Paul used the term "fathers" as a sign of courtesy and respect, just as St. Stephen did.

Rom. 4:11-12,18 - "So then, he [Abraham] is the *father* [emphasis added] of all who believe but have not been circumcised, in order that righteousness might be credited to them. And he is also the father of the circumcised who not only are circumcised but who also walk in the footsteps of the faith that our *father* [emphasis added] Abraham had before he was circumcised. . . . Against all hope, Abraham in hope believed and so became the *father* [emphasis added] of many nations. . . ."
Comment: St. Paul here refers to Abraham as the spiritual father of all who believe in Christ.

1 Cor. 4:14-15 - "I am not writing this to shame you, but to warn you, as my dear children. Even though you have ten thousand guardians in Christ, you do not have many fathers, for *in Christ Jesus I became your father through the Gospel*" [emphasis added].
Comment: Paul describes himself as the spiritual father of the Christians in Corinth (a Greek city where he established a faith community by preaching the Gospel).

1 Th. 2:11-12 - "For you know that we dealt with each of you *as a father deals with his own children* [emphasis added], encouraging, comforting you and urging you to live lives worthy of God, Who calls you into His kingdom and glory."

Comment: Again, Paul uses the word "father" to describe his role of leadership in the early Church.

Phlm 10 - "I appeal to you for my son Onesimus, who became my son while I was in chains."

Comment: In this passage, Paul refers to himself as the spiritual father of one of his converts.

Heb. 12:7,9 - "Endure hardship as a discipline; God is treating you as sons. For what son is not disciplined by his father? . . . Moreover, we have all had human fathers who disciplined us and we respected them for it. How much more should we submit to the Father of our spirits and live!"

Comment: Earthly fathers exercise authority as part of God's plan of salvation (though not to the same extent that He does)—so it is fitting that they also bear the title "father" (though again, their fatherhood is but a faint reflection of the Fatherhood of God).

1 Jn. 2:13-14 - "I write to you, fathers, because you have known Him Who is from the beginning. I write to you, young men, because you have overcome the evil one. I write to you, dear children, because you have known the Father. I write to you, fathers, because you have known Him Who is from the beginning."

Comment: St. John here refers to God as Father, and addresses earthly fathers in the same passage—showing that there is no conflict between the two ideas.

In Eph. 3:14-15 St. Paul states, "I kneel before the Father, from Whom His whole family in heaven and on earth derives its name." The Church is part of this family, and God has given its leaders the right to use the title "Father" as a sign of their vocation and their spiritual responsibilities and leadership. Let us pray that all those whom God has chosen in this way will live up to their calling.

SECTION D:

MARKS OF THE TRUE CHURCH

Chapter 16:

One, Holy, Catholic, Apostolic

A retired music teacher was visited by a friend who greeted him with the words, "What's the good news today?" In silent response, the music teacher got up, picked up a small hammer, and struck a tuning fork. Then, referring to the note whose sound still filled the room, he answered, "That note is an A. It is an A today; it was an A five thousand years ago; it will still be an A five thousand years from now. Sopranos may sing off key, tenors may go flat on their high notes, and pianos may be out of tune, but this note is forever an A—and that, my friend, is the good news today."

It is very good news that some things are predictable, reliable, and un-changing; otherwise, life would lack sanity, order, and meaning. Many people foolishly claim that truth is relative (in other words, "your truth" and "my truth" may be different and perhaps even contradictory), but even a cursory look at mathematics and the physical sciences invalidates this belief. The equations $2 + 2 = 4$ and $2 + 2 = 5$ cannot both be true; the consumption of a large dose of arsenic cannot simultaneously be poisonous to a human body and also the secret to good health; a tree cannot be a rock and a rock cannot be a tree. Something is, or it is not; all things created by God are (or, when free will comes into play, are meant to be) true to their nature. Since this is true in the lower, material realm, it's reasonable to believe it's also the case in the higher and more important spiritual realm—particularly in regard to the most crucial or significant spiritual question of all: the nature of salvation.

The Catholic Church has always claimed to be, and always will claim to be, the One True Church, and as such, the ordinary means of salvation for humanity. Jesus Christ, the Savior of the world, offers His life-giving grace through the Catholic Church in a unique, unprecedented, and indispensable way. This clear and divinely-inspired teaching cannot be both true and false (as in the belief that *all* paths lead to God, so it doesn't really matter which religion a person belongs to), for to claim that Christ's Church is necessary for the salvation of *some* people (i.e., Catholics alone), but not all, either means Christ's sacrificial death was unnecessary or incomplete, or that Jesus' promises to the apostles (Mt. 16:18-19; Lk.10:16; Jn. 14:16, etc.) were mistaken or deceptive.

Obviously no true Christian can accept either of these possibilities, for God is not contradictory or inconsistent (cf. 2 Cor. 1:18-19; Heb. 13:8)—especially not on a subject as vital as His children's eternal destiny. Therefore, His Son's one true Church must be clearly identifiable, possessing unmistakable "credentials" or reliable signs of her identity, available to all those who sincerely seek this knowledge and assurance.

The "marks" or identifying signs of the True Church are traditionally given as four: One, Holy, Catholic, and Apostolic. As the *Catechism of the Catholic Church* notes, the Church does not possess these qualities or characteristics of herself; rather, it is Christ, through the presence and activity of the Holy Spirit, Who makes the Church One, Holy, Catholic, and Apostolic (cf. par. 811). Moreover, "Only faith can recognize that the Church possesses these properties from her divine source. But their historical manifestations are signs that also speak clearly to human reason" (par. 812). In other words, even those who do not accept the Church's divine origin can, if intellectually honest, admit the logic and coherence of her claims.

One

After World War II, a U. S. Army chaplain who had been in a prisoner of war camp in Germany described Easter Mass as celebrated in the camp: "A saintly old French priest was the celebrant . . . I was the deacon, a Dutch priest was subdeacon, an Italian priest master of ceremonies, a Belgian was the thurifer, and for acolytes we had a Serb, a Scotsman, a Canadian, and a Russian. Two French priests directed and coordinated the choirs. . . . All the Catholics in the camp and many of the non-Catholics attended—the largest congregation I have ever seen apart from a national Eucharistic Congress. . . . Many of the Germans were there, not as guards, but as worshippers. . . . There was no argument here, no friction, no hatred, no intrigue or struggle for balance of power. Here was Christ being elevated again and drawing all things to Himself. Here was a King Whom all could love and obey, and in that love and obedience find the happiness and freedom and peace every man longs for."

This inspiring story illustrates the unity of the Church—a unity which transcends all national bounds and demonstrates the Church's oneness. To say that the Church is One means that she possesses visible bonds of communion or unity, including a profession of one faith, received from the apostles; a common celebration of divine worship, including the sacraments; and apostolic succession, or the handing-on of teaching authority from the apostles down through the ages to the present-day Pope and bishops (cf. *Catechism*, par. 813). The Church's unity—rooted in the Holy Spirit—is demonstrated by the fact that the opposition of the world, and the innumerable challenges she has faced over twenty centuries, have never succeeded in destroying her or forcing her to betray or deny her Lord or abandon her God-given mission.

Holy

Some year ago an Episcopalian minister observed, "Protestant churches make men stand up with their hands in the air and shout, but the Catholic Church makes men get down on their knees and pray." This perceived difference in styles of worship points not only to the Church's desire to help her members grow in grace, but also to her own fundamental holiness. The Church is holy, for as the Letter to the Ephesians tells us, Jesus gave Himself up for her so that "He might present to Himself the Church in splendor, without spot or wrinkle or any such thing, that she might be holy and without blemish" (5:27).

Only when the kingdom of God is fully established will all members of the Church be freed from every stain of sin; nevertheless, the Church on earth, though imperfect, already possesses a very real sanctity (cf. par. 825). One indication of this is the vast array of spiritual resources and opportunities for growth in personal sanctity offered to her members; in addition to a foundation of Scripture, Tradition, and the Sacraments, Catholics can choose from a wide variety of spiritualities and prayers and religious devotions. These, and the example of countless saints from every walk of life, are available to members of the Church seeking assis-tance on their own spiritual journey. St. Peter's role as keeper of the keys (cf. Mt. 16:19) means, among other things, that Jesus has entrusted to His Church the life-giving and nourishing spiritual riches individual believers need as they pursue holiness.

Catholic

As a youth, St. Augustine had belonged to the Manichean sect (which believed in two equally powerful gods, one good, and the other evil). He was later converted to Catholicism, in part because of the name "Catholic." He noted that no group separating itself from the Church could rightly claim that name: "For, though all lay claim to the title of Catholic, yet not one among them is called by that name, nor is there a heretic, who, if you met him on the street and asked him: 'Where is the Catholic Church?' would dare to direct you to his own schismatical church."

Even non-believers identify the Church of Rome (i.e., the religious body whose visible leader is the Pope) as Catholic—but this term is more than just a religious "brand name." According to the *Catechism*, "The word 'catholic' means 'universal,' in the sense of 'according to the totality' or 'in keeping with the whole'" (par. 830). Furthermore, the Church is catholic because Christ, the Lord of all creation, is present in her (cf. par. 830), and because He has commanded her to make disciples "of all nations" (Mt. 28:19).

Not only is Catholicism the largest Christian denomination, with over one billion members; the Church is also the only religious body in the world today that can rightly claim to transcend all national, societal, and cultural boundaries. Protestant denominations, including those with active missionary programs, are generally limited in their scope and influence, and the Orthodox Church—large as it is—has a negligible presence in many areas of the world. Even the vast and expanding reach of Islam (a non-Christian religion, of course, which denies the salvific power of Christ) falls short in comparison with Catholicism's international leadership, missionary out-reach, and universal outlook. Less than one hundred years after her founding, the Church was already known and referred to as "catholic"—and the accuracy of this identification remains unchanged today.

Apostolic

Early in the 20th century, when anti-Catholicism was still widespread in many parts of the United States, a young graduate from a teachers' college applied for a position in a Kansas school system. In the interview, the school board asked, among other things, the young man's religion, and he responded, "I belong to the First Christian Church." The board seemed satisfied with this answer, as the members wanted to be certain he wasn't a Catholic. Several weeks later, however, the superintendent confronted the new teacher by saying, "I'm hearing that you're attending a Catholic church every Sunday—but you told us you belong to the First Christian Church." The young man smiled and answered, "Sir, which is the First Christian Church? If I read history correctly, it's the Catholic Church, the one to which I belong." (Caught off guard, the angry superintendent muttered something about misrepresentation, but allowed the teacher to remain for the rest of the school year.)

Catholics can truthfully claim to belong to the "First Christian Church," for their Church existed before any other Christian religion. The term apostolic means that the Catholic Church—alone among all the more than 27,000 different Christian denominations—can trace her roots back to the apostles and to Jesus Himself. The Church is founded on the apostles in three ways: (1) by being built upon the foundation of St. Peter and his fellow apostles (Eph. 2:20; Rev. 21:14); (2) through the help of the Holy Spirit, Who assists her in keeping and handing on the teaching of the apostles; and (3) by continuing to be taught, sanctified, and guided by the apostles through their successors (cf. *Catechism*, par. 857).

Protestant denominations accept the authority of Scripture, but ignore or reject the Tradition through which Scripture was shaped, interpreted, and handed on; Orthodox Christians trace their roots back to the apostles, but downgrade or deny the fact that the Bishop of Rome (the Pope) shares in St. Peter's leadership and unique ministry of strengthening the brethren (cf. Lk. 22:32) and feeding Christ's flock (cf. Jn. 21:15ff). Only the Catholic Church avoids these inconsistencies and remains true to the vision of her Founder, and if the apostles were to return to earth today, they would recognize and fully approve of only those churches and individual Christians humbly submitting themselves to the authority and leadership of the successor of St. Peter.

Chapter 17:

Persecuted

The four traditional and official marks of the True Church are those examined in the previous chapter: One, Holy, Catholic, and Apostolic. However, it's possible to present four additional marks of the True Church. They're certainly not as important as the traditional marks of the Church, and because they're not official Church teaching, they fall in the realm of theological speculation. Nevertheless, they don't contradict the teaching of the Church, and they can serve a useful role in Catholic apologetics. (We might call them "secondary" marks, in order to distinguish them from the official, or "primary," marks.) One such secondary mark will be presented here, and a different one in each of the three chapters to follow.

The first secondary mark is that **the true Church is the one most fiercely attacked by Satan.** The Catholic Church is in the forefront of the ongoing spiritual war between good and evil; the Church has the most accurate understanding of the Enemy, and—through the Holy Spirit—the greatest degree of power over him.

Many churches have deliverance ministries or engage in some form of spiritual warfare, but none in such a formal way as Catholicism, which has, for instance, an official Rite of Exorcism and (at least in some dioceses) formally-appointed exorcists. (It's instructive that in the actual 1949 case of demonic possession on which the book and later the movie *The Exorcist* was based, the parents of the possessed boy took him to their Lutheran pastor for help; after his prayers failed to release the youth from spiritual bondage, the minister sent the family to a Catholic parish, saying that "Catholics are the ones who understand these things." The following year several priests successfully completed a long and grueling exorcism, and the teenager—now a man in his seventies—has since lived a quiet and uneventful life.)

Jesus called the devil "the prince of this world" (Jn. 12:31), and Satan jealously guards his evil kingdom, with his fiercest attacks directed at the Jews—God's original Chosen People—and at the Catholic Church, which St. Paul called the "true Israel of God" (Gal. 6:16). In regard to the Church, the devil is constantly trying to stir up persecution, opposition, ridicule, heresy, religious dissent, pride, disobedience, misunderstanding, division, factionalism, fear, doubt, and confusion—for any and all of these evils advances Satan's goals and makes it harder for the Church to fulfill her mission.

In 1884 Pope Leo XIII had a famous vision in which the devil boasted that, given sufficient time, he could destroy the Church; Jesus granted him the opportunity, but promised that the Church would emerge from the ordeal more powerful and glorious than before. (It was this terrifying vision that prompted the Pope to compose the prayer to St. Michael the Archangel.)

Some commentators have suggested that Satan's assault against the Church over the last 120 years has had two targets in particular: family life and the priesthood. We've certainly witnessed a breakdown in family life, with painful results for the Church and disastrous consequences for American society, and the recent terrible scandals in the priesthood are undeniable proof that the devil has had some major successes in this area, too (though this is not to excuse the guilty priests or bishops or to deny their personal responsibility for their grave sins against God's children).

Many experts believe the scandal of sexual abuse is at least as widespread and severe in certain Protestant denominations (besides being many times worse in the government-run school system) as it is in the Catholic Church—leading to the question of why there's little hue and cry about those equally sinful situations. Part of the answer is that Satan isn't as concerned about those other Christian denominations as he is about Catholicism; from his point of view, it makes sense to concentrate his attacks on his greatest enemy.

Above and beyond that, however, it may well be that Jesus is letting His One True Church undergo the painful, humbling, but absolutely necessary process of being purified and cleansed—whereas He's allowing some other Christian churches to continue on their path to increasing irrelevancy and decline. We as Catholics may be witnessing an important "sorting out" process, in which the true Church is becoming like gold tested by fire (cf. 1 Pt. 1:7) in preparation for her final victory over evil.

Chapter 18

Prophetic

If the first secondary mark of the true Church is that it's the one most opposed, or persecuted, by the devil, the next secondary mark is that **the true Church is willing to take unpopular positions.** In the Old Testament, this was frequently the sign of genuine prophecy; for instance, Elijah was the only servant of God opposing the 450 prophets of Baal (1 Kgs. 18:22), the message of Amos was rejected by the nation of Israel (Am. 7:12-13), and Jeremiah was arrested and threatened with death for warning that national sinfulness would lead to defeat and disgrace (Jer. 20: 7; 26:8).

This theme of worldly opposition to the truth is further developed in the New Testament, particularly in St. John's Gospel, which presents Jesus as the light of the world (8:12), a light the darkness has unsuccessfully tried to extinguish (1:5). Sinners prefer to remain in darkness so their evil deeds go unexposed (3:20)—and as a result, they will naturally oppose those who shine the light of truth in their direction. Followers of Jesus are not of this world (17:16), and so, like Him, they can expect persecution for their efforts to witness to the truth (15:20-21).

Thus, unpopularity is seemingly part of the Christian's job description — and, as even a casual observer will note, the religion which is "best" at making itself unpopular with the world is Catholicism. Part of the reason for this is size: the largest Church will obviously have the most opportunities for being involved in controversy. However, a much more important reason for Catholicism's unpopularity is the fact that it upholds strict, unchanging moral values—values which are often diametrically opposed to those lifestyles and beliefs promoted by the world.

This is most especially true in the area of sexual morality, where the Church continues her traditional defense of the sanctity of marriage—a teaching which rules out fornication, adultery, homosexual activity, pornography, and various forms of "pleasure" popular with many people. Catholicism is quite willing to be dismissed as "behind the times" in this regard, for it's her mission to preach God's unchanging truth in season and out of season (cf. 1 Tim. 4:2), even at the risk of opposing popular culture. (Upholding the 6th Commandment—which forbids sexual immorality—is an especially important mission entrusted to the Church in terms of the salvation of souls, for in her apparitions at Fatima, Our Lady revealed that more persons are in Hell for sexual sins than for any other kind.)

The Church is also known for her unyielding opposition to abortion, euthanasia, embryonic stem cell research and manipulation, genetic cloning, and various other unwarranted scientific and medical experiments. Catholicism is not opposed to legitimate research and experimentation, and has traditionally been very supportive of such things (as chapter 21 will show); however, the Church consistently warns that instead of treating Science and Progress with godlike reverence, society must ensure that these things remain humanity's servants and do not become ends in themselves (cf. *Catechism,* par. 2293).

Furthermore, the Holy Father, different Congregations of the Roman Curia (speaking in the Pope's name), and certain national bishops' conferences, have spoken extensively on issues of war and peace, economic justice, capital punishment, racism, and various other subjects—including some (e.g., a refusal to ordain women) involving the life of the Church herself. Even the fiercest critic of Catholicism must admit that the Church is not afraid to take unpopular positions.

No other Christian religion can claim the same degree of moral consistency and fidelity, especially in the face of societal opposition and scorn, as Catholicism. The classic example of this, of course, involves artificial contraception ("birth control"), the rejection of which can be traced back to the earliest traditions of Christianity. (For instance, contraception is forbidden in the 1st century Christian writing known as the *Didache,* or "Teaching.")

Until 1930, *every Christian denomination* was united in condemning the use of birth control; Luther, Calvin, Zwingli, and the other Protestant leaders had—like the Catholic Church—denounced it as a grave sin. Then, at its Lambeth Conference in 1930, the Anglican church decided to make an exception for married couples who had a "sufficiently serious reason" for contracepting. (This breach of Christian tradition was condemned by Pope Pius XI in his encyclical *Casti Connubii,* which appeared the following year.)

Human nature being what it is, one exception to this traditional prohibition of contraception (like a small leak in the "dike of morality") led to another, and then to another, and so on—and before long, the original moral principle had disappeared or become unrecognizable. Soon other Protestant churches began going along with the times, eventually leaving

Catholicism virtually alone in remaining faithful to the earliest teachings and practices of Christianity.

Many people expected this situation to change when, shortly before his death, Pope John XXIII appointed a commission to review the Church's teaching on the issue of contraception. However, in his 1968 encyclical *Humanae Vitae,* John's successor, Pope Paul VI—knowing full well that it would stir up bitter opposition—reaffirmed the Church's traditional teaching. (In retrospect, it's clear the Holy Father's encyclical was inspired by the Holy Spirit, for all the evils the Pope warned against if the use of artificial contraception became widespread—including an increase in divorce, abortion, and child and spousal abuse—have multiplied disastrously.)

Truth has always been unpopular—and Catholicism has always been willing to risk unpopularity by proclaiming and defending the truth. The quote of Archbishop Fulton J. Sheen given in chapter 4 is worth repeating here: "If the grace of God did not give me the fullness of Truth, and I were looking for it, I would begin my search by looking through the world for a Church that did not get along with the evil in the world! If that Church [were] accused of countless lies, hated because it refused to compromise, ridiculed because it refused to fit the times . . . , I would suspect that since it was hated by what is evil in the world, it was therefore good and holy; and if it is good and holy, it must be Divine."

Chapter 19:

Saintly

So far we've seen that the One True Church is *persecuted* and *prophetic*. A third secondary mark is that **many of its members will go "above and beyond the call of duty" in living out their faith.** Jesus spoke of the good seed that produced at a rate of thirty or sixty or a hundred-fold (Mk. 4:20), and the history of Catholicism shows us many such examples.

Every Christian denomination, of course, has many adherents who are truly committed to Christ, even to the point of dying for their faith, if necessary—and their fidelity and service are very pleasing to the Lord, and a glorious sign for all humanity of the truth of the Gospel. However, when it comes to practicing the faith not only in a committed way, but in a truly heroic and outstanding manner, no other religion can compare to Catholicism in the sheer breadth, depth, and number of its saints.

(This secondary mark of saintliness is in some ways very similar to one of the official marks of the True Church, but a distinction can be made between the two. The entire Church is, and will be made, *holy* as the spotless Bride of Christ, referred to in Eph. 5:27 and Rev. 21:2; the idea of *saintliness* is more a description of many individual members of the Church.)

Some of the greatest and most inspirational figures of all human history belonged to the Catholic Church, including St. Peter, St. Paul, all the other apostles, St. Mary Magdalene, St. Augustine, St. Leo, St. Gregory, St. Francis of Assisi, St. Catherine of Siena, St. Thérèse of Lisieux, and, of course, the greatest saint of all: the Virgin Mary. (Some people might object to the Church's exclusive claim to Mary and the apostles, but Acts 1:13-14 and 2:1 places them together at the "birthday" or beginning of the Church, when the Holy Spirit descended on the feast of Pentecost; moreover, as St. Paul makes clear in 1 Cor. 1:10-13, the idea of competing groups or factions within Christianity was deeply foreign and disturbing to him and the other early Church leaders.)

The Catholic Church (and also the Orthodox Church, though not to the same degree) has a formal and rigorous process for determining which of its many very holy members are worthy of the title "Saint," and this process has resulted in the canonization of men, women, and children from every era of Christian history and from virtually every nationality, race, culture, and way of life. More than any other religion, Catholicism recognizes our human need for role models, and responds to this need abundantly. For virtually every profession, the Church is able to offer a patron saint; for every one of life's challenges and problems, the Church can point to the example of saints who faced it and, with God's help, overcame it.[1]

Among the thousands of saints honored by the Church, we find royalty and commoners, the rich and poor, young and old, weak and powerful, learned and uneducated; Catholicism's "Hall of Fame" includes popes and maidens, warriors and missionaries, mystics and teachers, clergy and lay persons, martyrs and virgins, married couples and parents, and people of every imaginable background, talent, and personality type. No two saints were exactly alike, but all of them shared a burning love for Jesus Christ and an unshakeable loyalty to the Church He established.

Catholic saints have performed amazing miracles, cheerfully endured unimaginable burdens and hardships, made thousands of converts, changed the course of history, and borne witness to Christ in innumerable wonderful and inspiring ways. Other Christians have their heroes, too, but for every Albert Schweitzer produced by Protestantism, Catholicism has a dozen Mother Teresas and Brother Damiens.

The spiritual heights reached by many of the Church's canonized saints are unparalleled—but this is what we would expect from the only Church able to nourish her children's spiritual growth with all seven Sacraments, particularly the Eucharist and Reconciliation. Jesus tells us that "by their fruits you will know them" (Mt. 7:20), and so the ability of the Church to raise up saintly figures again and again throughout history is an unmistakable sign of Catholicism's divine origin and the Holy Spirit's ongoing presence.

Chapter 20:

Miraculous

To the three secondary marks of the One True Church we've examined so far—*persecuted, prophetic,* and *saintly*—we can a fourth and final one: **The One True Church will demonstrate many signs of the miraculous.** The Gospels tell us that Jesus worked numerous miracles during His public ministry (Mk. 1:34, 6:56, etc.), and in the early Church, many signs and wonders were performed by the apostles (Acts 2:43). Therefore, any church claiming to be acting under the authority of Christ and His apostles should also be able to point to frequent instances of the miraculous working of divine power.

The Catholic Church, all throughout her history, has been able to do this—not only in terms of the miracles performed by her leaders and members (many of them canonized saints), but also by means of various events which can only have a supernatural origin. No other religion has witnessed so many scientifically-inexplicable wonders; no other church has been entrusted with so many proofs (to those with open minds) of God's presence and power.

One of the most striking examples of this was the "Miracle of the Sun," an amazing celestial display promised several months earlier by Our Lady at Fatima in Portugal (and it remains the only recorded instance in history of a successful prediction of the exact date of a miracle). On October 13, 1917, a crowd of some 70,000 people waiting in a steady rain for the promised event observed the noonday sun appear. To their amazement, the sun suddenly began to "dance" back and forth across the sky, change colors while spinning rapidly, and then seemingly plunge toward the earth (filling the onlookers with terror), before resuming its normal place.

Those present were able to stare directly at the sun during this display without harm to their eyes, and discovered afterwards that their clothes and the ground on which they were standing, previously soaked by the rain, were now completely dry. (The Portuguese newspapers, even though anti-Catholic, reported the events of October 13 honestly and accurately.) The three young visionaries to whom Mary appeared were Catholic; her messages supported the authority of the Catholic Church, and it was the Catholic Church which investigated the apparitions at Fatima and declared them to be "worthy of belief."

Another famous miracle involving an apparition of Our Lady took place in 1531 near present-day Mexico City. Mary sent an Indian named Juan Diego to the local bishop with a sign: not only a bouquet of roses (which in Mexico don't bloom in December), but an imprint of her image miraculously infused on Juan's tilma, or cloak. Almost 500 years later, the image hasn't yet faded, and scientists are unable to explain how it was created. Moreover, closer examination has even shown that reflections of the bishop and the people with him when Juan Diego opened the tilma can be seen on Our Lady's eyes—just as such images would be reflected in the eyes of a living person.

The Catholic Church has witnessed, or been the recipient of, many other amazing signs and miracles. In the Italian town of Lanciano in the 8th century, for instance, a priest doubted whether the consecrated bread and wine truly became the Body and Blood of Christ; as he elevated the Host during Mass, it thereupon turned into an actual piece of human flesh. This miraculous flesh, and the drops of blood that appeared with it, are preserved to this day, and scientific studies have confirmed their authenticity as human flesh and blood.

Also, the dried blood of St. Januarius, a 4th century martyr, liquefies eighteen times a year without any visible cause; various experiments have been conducted by scientists, but none have explained the phenomenon. Numerous other wonders include the bodies of several saints remaining incorrupt (that is, staying lifelike in appearance instead of decomposing) many years after their deaths; certain saints, beginning with Francis of Assisi, suddenly receiving the stigmata (bleeding wounds similar to those suffered by Christ on the Cross) without medical explanation; and documented instances of the miraculous multiplication of food, prolonged or permanent fasting, levitation, and bilocation on the part of Catholic saints.

One of the most amazing miracles of all—and one of the most compelling, as it occurred fairly recently—involves the only two uses of atomic weapons in history so far. On the morning of August 6, 1945, four Jesuit priests and four lay persons were in the church of Our Lady of the Assumption in the Japanese city of Hiroshima, praying the Rosary at the exact moment the atomic bomb was detonated. The center of the nuclear explosion was a mere eight blocks away, yet not one of the eight Catholics was killed, wounded, or even affected by radiation (even though 90% of the city was destroyed and 130,000 people were killed or wounded). Over

200 scientists examined these survivors during the following years, but no one had a medical or scientific explanation of their seemingly impossible survival.[2]

Three days after Hiroshima was destroyed, a second atomic weapon was dropped on the Japanese city of Nagasaki, resulting in some 75,000 people killed or wounded. Once again, a handful of Catholics—a group of Franciscan friars—happened to be in the center of the explosion, and emerged unscathed. They attributed their miraculous preservation to the fact that they too were living the message of Fatima (a call to offer prayers and acts of penance for peace in the world and the conversion of sinners).

Signs and events such as these aren't always widely known or reported, but in most cases, they have been verified and documented beyond any reasonable doubt. The Catholic Church has been entrusted with these and many other wonders and miracles (and while it's true that Satan can to a certain degree perform false wonders and signs, God never allows a permanent deception of those genuinely seeking the truth—which means that the on-going and authentically miraculous signs possessed by Catholicism can only be miraculous in origin).

In a somewhat different context, St. James challenges us, "Demonstrate your faith to me without works, and I will demonstrate my faith to you from my works" (Jas. 2:18). The Catholic Church has always been able to meet this challenge; she not only believes in miracles, but—through the Holy Spirit—also performs and possesses them, and in this way gives yet another sign that she is the One True Church of Jesus Christ.

Thus, in addition to recognizing that the True Church is one, holy, catholic, and apostolic, we can say that it possesses four other, unofficial, or "secondary" marks of authenticity. The True Church is the one most fiercely attacked by Satan, the one most willing to challenge the world by taking unpopular positions, the one that enables many of its members to advance far beyond the normal degree of holiness, and the one giving the clearest witness to God's powerful and mysterious presence in the world. We can summarize these four secondary marks of the One True Church as **persecuted, prophetic, saintly,** and **miraculous**—and only the Catholic Church truly embodies all these descriptions in their fullness.

Jesus Christ is the fullness of all that is holy and true (Jn. 1:16; Eph. 1:23; Col. 1:19), and He is the same yesterday, today, and forever (Heb. 13:8)—so it's only natural and logical that His One True Church continues to proclaim His unchanging Gospel in all its fullness. As the ordinary means of salvation for all humanity, the Catholic Church is God's great gift to the world and an essential part of his eternal plan of redemption—and the signs or marks verifying this claim are there for all who wish to find them.

CHRIST'S CHURCH — PAST, PRESENT, AND FUTURE

Chapter 21:

Common Historical Myths

Any institution with a 2000-year history, and with as many enemies and critics as Catholicism, will—rightly or wrongly—often find itself on the defensive. Because of the sinfulness of her leaders and members, the Church—while infallibly preserving the truths necessary for salvation—has sometimes given scandal, missed opportunities, or failed to live up to her Founder's teachings and standards. As the *Catechism* acknowledges,

> Christ, "holy, innocent, and undefiled," knew nothing of sin, but came only to expiate the sins of the people. The Church, however, clasping sinners to her bosom, at once holy and always in need of purification, follows constantly the path of penance and renewal. All members of the Church, including her ministers, must acknowledge that they are sinners" (par. 827).

The Catholic Church, particularly under the leadership of Pope John Paul II, set an example of honesty and integrity for all religions by humbly acknowledging her historical failings and seeking forgiveness from persons and groups sinned against or harmed by her members. However, as the Pope observed, it often seemed that Catholics were the only ones apologizing, even though virtually all major religions—Christian and non-Christian—have at one time or another been guilty of sins against God and humanity.

The One True Church has nothing to fear from admitting her failings, for she has the assurance of being "consecrated in truth" (cf. Jn. 17:17). Such openness and humility, however, does not require allow her to "turn the other cheek" when it comes to defending and explaining the truths entrusted to her by Christ. Rather, she must light her light shine before all (cf. Mt. 5:14-16), and this often requires individual Catholics to defend her against false accusations.

There are many myths about the Church, ideas exaggerated or taken out of context in an effort to discredit Catholicism; even though such myths have little factual basis, some Protestants (or non-Christians, or atheists) attempt to use them as "gotcha" moments in their discussions with unprepared and defensive Catholics. Therefore, it's important for members of the Church to know something about her history[1] and to be ready to defend her against unjust accusations. Four such common historical myths are presented here.

Catholicism vs. Science[2]

It's widely believed that the Catholic Church has consistently opposed, or at the very least considered suspect, scientific inquiry and progress — but in fact, just the opposite is the case. Indeed, without Judeo-Christian thought, the existence of science as we know it would be impossible.

Many great ancient cultures (the Arabic, Babylonian, Chinese, Egyptian, Greek, Hindu, and Mayan) viewed history as a constantly repeating cycle of death and rebirth, and destruction and renewal, thereby preventing any real sense of progress or development — for if nothing ever permanently changed, there was little point in working for long-lasting improvements in the human condition. Also, ancient peoples often viewed created things (rocks, trees, volcanoes, heavenly bodies, etc.) as having minds and wills of their own, capable of arbitrary behavior; this ruled out any sense of predictability, which is an absolutely essential element of science. (Certainly these ancient cultures had some impressive achievements, but they lacked any sort of formal and ongoing scientific application or inquiry.)

The Jewish, and later Catholic, belief in linear history — in which all human history, rather than recycling endlessly, has a definite beginning, end, and purpose — along with the insistence that all created things are subject to a rational created order established by an unchanging Creator, makes possible the process of experimentation and discovery on which science depends. Scientific inquiry requires an intelligent, orderly world (for if an experiment conducted one day produces a certain result, and the exact same experiment conducted under the exact same conditions the following day produces a different result, the realm of science is replaced by magic). Catholicism insists that such an intelligent, orderly world does exist; moreover, God has commanded us to unlock its secrets by exerciseing responsible stewardship over it (cf. Gen. 1:28).

Rather than opposing education and discovery—whether in science or any other field—the Church has vigorously supported such endeavors. It was the Church, for instance, which created universities as we now know them, with faculties, courses of study, examinations, and the awarding of formal degrees, and which promoted other types of education (within the limits imposed by various difficulties and crises) and which strove to preserve the learning and culture of earlier societies. Church leaders were often patrons of scientific inquiry, and a number of cathedrals (such as those in Bologna, Florence, Paris, and Rome) were intentionally designed as world-class solar observatories (facilitating astronomical study).

Critics are quick to point to the Church's "persecution" of the astronomer Galileo Galilei (and to John Paul II's apology for the Church's role in this controversy) as proof that Catholicism is opposed to scientific inquiry. Aside from the fact that this is virtually the *only* historical example they can cite, the truth is simply that the Church didn't object to the hypothesis of the earth revolving around the sun in itself, but merely to Galileo's insistence that the hypothesis was an established fact, when in fact it had not yet been proven as such. (Personality issues, and Church sensitivity to Protestant accusations that Catholics didn't pay sufficient attention to Scriptural passages suggesting a stationary earth, also entered into the equation.)

Not only have some great scientists, such as Louis Pasteur, been devout Catholics; many important scientists have been Catholic priests, including Roger Bacon (the forerunner of the modern scientific method), St. Albert the Great (who in the 13th century noted the importance of learning about the created world through direct observation), Robert Grosseteste (the first man to write down a complete set of steps for performing a scientific experiment), Giambattista Riccioli (the first scientist to determine the rate of acceleration of a freely falling body), Roger Boscovich (the originator of fundamental atomic physics), and Athanasius Kircher (whose work in the field of chemistry helped debunk the myth of alchemy).

Catholic scholars made vital discoveries in the fields of mathematics, geometry, optics, biology, geomagnetism, meteorology, solar physics, and geology; the contributions of Jesuits (members of the Society of Jesus) in the field of seismology were so great that it's sometimes referred to as "the Jesuit science." Jesuit scholars also performed the valuable work of recording their experimental results in encyclopedias (immensely aiding the spread of scientific knowledge), and were the first to introduce Western science to places such as India and China.

Thus, the Church's contributions to science have been significant, and Catholics have little reason to be ashamed or defensive in this regard.

"Bloody Mary" vs. "Good Queen Bess": An Honest Comparison

Because the Church refused to annul his marriage to Catherine of Aragon, King Henry VIII declared himself to be "Head of the Church in England" and led the English church into schism (thereby establishing what eventually became known as the Anglican church). Many Church properties were seized by the Crown (causing grave harm to the poor who relied upon the Church's charity), and almost 650 Catholics who opposed Henry's repression of the Church (including the bishop St. John Fisher, and his own royal chancellor, St. Thomas More) were executed.

Henry's daughter Mary I, whose mother was Catherine of Aragon, was a devout Catholic; during her reign (1553-58) she attempted to restore Catholicism. Mary arrested and executed Protestant leaders, such as Thomas Cramner (her father's heretical archbishop), who had either opposed her accession to the throne or afterwards plotted against her; this was the origin of the "Bloody Mary" legend, which was largely created and promoted by the anti-Catholic author of Foxe's *Book of Martyrs*.[3]

Of the 273 "martyrs" listed in this book of Protestant propaganda, however, 169 were most likely criminals who would have been executed regardless of who ruled England at the time. The remaining 104 executions occurred for religious reasons—something we in 21st century America, with our background of religious freedom and toleration, quite understandably view as indefensible and extreme. It should be remembered, however, that in opposing Mary—the legitimate Queen of England—these Protestants were guilty of treason, which even today is considered a capital offense. Also, considerably fewer people were executed under Mary than under her father or her half-sister Elizabeth.

Though popular with most of her subjects, Mary's reign was short, as she became deathly ill after only five years as Queen. Her rightful heir to the English throne was Mary Stuart ("Mary Queen of Scots"), but because this Mary was married to the heir to the French throne, Queen Mary's husband, Phillip II of Spain, urged her for political reasons to name Elizabeth, Henry's illegitimate daughter by his mistress Anne Boleyn, as her heir. Mary did not trust Elizabeth, but when the young woman solemnly promised that she would continue the restoration of the Catholic Church in England, the dying queen designated her as her successor.

In 1558 Elizabeth I ("Elizabeth the Great") began her 45 year reign; while it was a time of cultural flowering and some notable foreign policy successes, it was also an era of, first repression, and then outright persecution, of Catholicism. Elizabeth almost immediately went back on her promise to Mary, deciding—primarily for political reasons—to promote Protestantism in her realm. She restored the Act of Supremacy (her father's declaration that he was supreme in all religious matters in England), along with the Book of Common Prayer (introduced by Thomas Cramner), rejected the Catholic Mass and priesthood, and replaced virtually all the English bishops with others consecrated according to an invalid formula.[4]

Increasingly stern measures were enacted against Catholics. Mass was outlawed, and fines were levied against persons refusing to attend Anglican services. Anyone caught secretly attending Mass (as many Catholics did) could be fined or imprisoned, and such persons were forced to take the Oath of Supremacy; a refusal to do so risked the death penalty. Bringing Catholic religious items into the country was declared illegal, and informers were paid to report on the activities of Catholics, especially priests—who were liable to execution as traitors. The reconciliation of Anglicans to the True Church was also considered treason.

During Elizabeth's long reign, 189 English Catholics were martyred; she was also responsible for the deaths of hundreds more Catholics in Ireland. Thus, the historical record strongly suggests that it's Elizabeth, not Mary, who should be known to history as the "Bloody Queen of England." That there were many Catholics willing to risk death under her reign speaks well of Catholicism, and the testimony of one of them—St. Edmund Campion—expresses very clearly the inherent contradiction in Elizabeth's religious policies. Addressing the court which would sentence him to death, he stated, "In condemning us [Catholics] you condemn all your own ancestors—all the ancient priests, bishops, and kings—all that was once the glory of England, the island of saints, and the most devoted child of the See of Peter. For what have we taught, however you may qualify it with the odious name of treason, that they did not uniformly teach?"

Ultimately, of course, it's not the judgment of history that matters, but the judgment of God—and in this regard, the manner of death of the two queens is very instructive. Queen Mary died a holy, peaceful death, spiritually nourished and reconciled to God through the Church's Sacraments. Elizabeth, however, in her final, agonizing months, was terrified of death. She tried to avoid sleeping (fearing she might not awake), resisted the ministrations of Anglican priests, and desperately tried to delay the inevitable—perhaps suggesting a justified fear of divine judgment.

The Truth About the Spanish Inquisition[5]

If you were to be held accountable, and possibly put on trial, for your religious beliefs, under which of these systems would you prefer to be examined?

Under the first system, you would be subject to a civil and religious authority professing a faith different from your own, and might be arrested and imprisoned without being informed of your accusers or even of the charges against you. Moreover, while in prison, you could be forbidden all communication with your family, denied legal counsel and the chance to speak in your own defense, and—without a trial ever being held—found guilty of treason or other crimes, resulting in either the loss of all your property, permanent imprisonment, or even death.

Under the second system, you would only be subject to the civil and religious authorities if you claimed to be the same religion as them, and if accused of a religious crime, you'd be granted a one month "period of grace" for repentance—and if you repented, only a mild penance (never a severe one) would be imposed. If you insisted on a trial, you'd be asked to write a list of all your enemies, and their testimony would be disqualified from being used against you. You'd be assisted by trained lawyers, and if you objected to a particular judge, he'd be removed from the case. Witnesses against you would have to be in substantial agreement for a guilty verdict to be rendered, and severe penalties would be imposed upon anyone giving false testimony against you. If you were found guilty, there would be a chance of execution, but this penalty would be very unlikely; the punishment would probably be much milder—perhaps only a reprimand or a public act of penance.

If you had to choose between these two legal systems, which would you prefer? Obviously, the second—which means you'd choose to be judged under the rules and methods of the Spanish Inquisition, as opposed to the rule of law in England under King Henry VIII and his daughter Queen Elizabeth I.

Contrary to popular belief, the Spanish Inquisition was not an unbridled religious persecution resulting in the deaths of thousands of people whose only crime was seeking the freedom to worship God as they chose. A relatively high degree of religious toleration existed in Spain (due to the presence of thousands of Jews and Moors, or Muslims), and the Inquisition did nothing to change this. Instead, it was intended to address the heresies and immoral behavior of many false converts to Catholicism.

At the request of the Bishop of Osama, Pope Sixtus IV established the Inquisition in 1478—and limited its jurisdiction to persons claiming to be Catholic. Because its purpose was to ensure the preservation of authentic Catholic doctrine (something the Church had every right to do), Jews and Muslims were specifically exempted from its authority and decrees. Such was the Inquisition's reputation that persons accused of other crimes, when given a choice, invariably preferred to be examined by the judges of the Inquisition, rather than those of the royal courts.

The vast majority of the persons brought before the Spanish Inquisition were either found innocent, or assigned a mild penance as a way of absolving them from their sins and reconciling them to the Church. Contrary to the popular image, torture—which was used quite commonly throughout Europe—was very infrequently resorted to by the Inquisition (though, of course, our modern outlook requires that it not be used at all).

Also, the number of persons put to death by the Inquisition is far less than commonly supposed. According to information given in a documentary presented by the BBC, "There were more men and women executed in one day during the French Revolution than the Spanish Inquisition handed over to execution during the entire 16th century." Indeed, no more than fifty people suffered the death penalty in Spain during that entire 100-year period, whereas in England Henry VIII executed hundreds of Catholics (without any of the legal safeguards observed by the Inquisition), and his daughter Elizabeth I created more victims than the Spanish and Roman Inquisitions together over the course of three centuries.

We can certainly lament the fact that perhaps 5000 people were killed in the 350 years the Spanish Inquisition was in operation—but to keep this in perspective, it must be remembered that during the same period, 150,000 alleged witches were executed throughout the rest of Europe. Also, because of its vigorous search for the truth of each case, the Inquisition helped prevent the persecution of innocent people—something that happened quite frequently elsewhere in Europe and in the New World (e.g., the Salem Witch Trials).

As noted by the above-mentioned BBC documentary, the myth of the terrible Spanish Inquisition was "conjured up by Catholic Spain's Protestant enemies when it was apparent they could not defeat Spain on the battlefield." Today we finally know the truth: The Inquisition may not be a cause for pride, but it's certainly not a cause for shame.

Was Pope Pius XII "silent" about the Jews?[6]

Several recent books have attempted to argue that during World War II, Pope Pius XII (and by implication, the Catholic Church) knew about the Nazis' extermination campaign against the Jewish people, and deliberately turned a blind eye, instead of protesting and opposing this terrible evil. Examples of this revisionist history include *Constantine's Sword* by James Carroll; *Papal Sin*, by Gary Wills; *Under His Very Windows*, by Susan Zuccotti; and perhaps the most infamous of all, *Hitler's Pope*, by John Cornwell. However, these works have all been refuted and discredited by unbiased scholarship (and Mr. Cornwell has since acknowledged some of the serious flaws in his book).

The "case" against Pius XII can only be made by ignoring some very important, but (for the Church's critics) inconvenient facts:

As Secretary of State for Pius XI, Eugenio Cardinal Pacelli (the future Pius XII) played a key role in formulating and implementing the Vatican's policy of opposition to Nazi Germany — a policy which became increasingly more outspoken as the true nature of the Nazi regime became apparent. For instance, the 1937 papal encyclical *Mit brennender Sorge (With Burning Anxiety)*, in which Pius XI condemned the new paganism represented by Nazi Germany, was actually drafted by Cardinal Pacelli.

When Cardinal Pacelli was elected Pope early in 1939, the German government was very upset because, as an editorial in the *Berlin Morgenpost* stated, "he was always opposed to Naziism." That October, one month after World War II began with Germany's invasion of Poland, Pius XII's first encyclical, *Summi Pontificatus*, condemned aggressive warfare. This delighted the British (who gave it wide publicity), but outraged the Nazis (who arrested German priests brave enough to read it from the pulpit).

In January 1940, at the Pope's instruction, *L'Osservatore Romano* (the Vatican's official newspaper) and Vatican radio first revealed to the world the terrible treatment of Jews and Catholics were suffering in occupied Poland at the hands of their German conquerors. Furthermore, in his Christmas messages of 1941 and 1942, the Pope protested the actions of the Nazis and expressed support for their victims. In response, the *New York Times* editorialized, "The voice of Pope Pius XII is a lonely voice in the silence and darkness enveloping Europe this Christmas. . . . In calling for a 'real new order' based on 'liberty, justice, and love' . . . the Pope put himself squarely against Hitlerism."

When the Catholic bishops of Holland bravely protested the Nazi persecution of the Jews in their country, the Germans responded by deporting and eventually murdering a larger percentage of Jews from Holland (79%) than from any other Western European nation. Pius XII had been preparing an even stronger and more direct denunciation of Hitler's regime—but when he heard what happened after the Church's futile protest in Holland, he tore up the document to avoid provoking an even worse Nazi reaction against the Jewish people. From then on he remained "silent" while actively opposing the Nazis behind the scenes—the same prudent and quietly heroic approach used by the International Red Cross.

The Pope had been strongly urged by Jewish leaders and by Catholic bishops in German-occupied countries not to protest the Nazi crimes publicly, as this would only make things worse. An Italian Jew in Rome stated twenty years after the war, "None of us wanted the Pope to speak out openly. . . . The Gestapo would only have increased and intensified its inquisition . . . it was much better the Pope kept silent. We all felt the same, and today we still believe that." Moreover, a bishop from Luxembourg, who had himself been an inmate in the Dachau concentration camp for eighteen months, notified the Vatican on his release that "whenever protests were made, treatment of prisoners worsened immediately."

When the Germans occupied Rome in 1943, they threatened severe reprisals against the city's Jews unless they paid a ransom of 50 kilograms of gold within 24 hours. There was no way to collect this much gold—until Pius directed that some of the Vatican's gold chalices be melted down for this purpose. The Pope also ordered all the convents, seminaries, monasteries, and schools of Rome (155 different institutions) to hide Jewish refugees—and 3000 were hidden at the papal summer home of Castel Gandolfo. Pius also used his family fortune to help smuggle Jews across German lines, and he had the Vatican issue safe-conduct passes and even fake baptismal certificates to Jews seeking to escape.

The German ambassador to the Vatican, Ernst von Weizsacker, told his superiors in Berlin that the Pope was not interfering in German efforts to round up Italian Jews—apparently the "smoking gun" or proof revisionist historians need to make their case against Pius XII. However, the fact is that Weizsacker, who was sympathetic to the Church and the Jews, knew that Hitler would order the Vatican invaded if he learned the truth—and in order to prevent this, the ambassador deliberately misled the Nazi regime.

In a 1944 interview with *Time* magazine, the great scientist Albert Einstein said that once the Nazis came to power in Germany, "Only the [Catholic] Church stood squarely across the path of Hitler's godless campaign. I never had any special interest in the Church before, but now I feel a great admiration. I am forced to confess that what I once despised, I now praise unreservedly."

Pius XII received similar praise once the war was ended; he was officially thanked for his efforts on behalf of persecuted Jews by the Emergency Committee to Save the Jewish People of Europe, the World Jewish Congress, the American Jewish Congress, Agudas Israel World Organization, and the War Refugee Board; moreover, when the chief rabbi of Rome, Israel Zolli, converted to Catholicism after the war, he chose Eugenio as his baptismal name as a way of honoring the Pope.

In 1955 the Israeli Philharmonic Orchestra gave a special performance at the Vatican's Consistory Hall as an official expression of Israel's gratitude for the Pope's efforts on behalf of the Jews, and when Pius XII died in 1958, he was praised by numerous international Jewish organizations and leaders—including Golda Meir (then Israel's Minister of Foreign Affairs) and the chief rabbi of Palestine.

Israeli historian and diplomat Pinchas Lapide, in his 1967 book *Three Popes and the Jews* (still considered the definitive Jewish study of the Nazi Holocaust), wrote that Pope Pius XII "was instrumental in saving at least 700,000, but probably as many as 860,000 Jews from certain death at Nazi hands" (including 200,000 in Hungary, 50,000 in Poland, 360,000 in Bulgaria, and 250,000 in Rumania).

Aside from Communist critics of the Church (attempting to discredit the Church in postwar Italy), *no one* accused Pius XII of "indifference" to the fate of the Jews . . . until 1963, when a German Protestant named Rolf Hochhuth wrote a play called "The Deputy," which portrayed the Pope as being indirectly complicit in the Holocaust. Within a few short decades, this *fictional play* somehow (diabolical disorientation?) achieved greater credibility than all the documented facts listed here, and this vicious slander quickly took on a life of its own (often promoted by Church critics with a hidden agenda of their own).

Could the Church have done even more than it did during World War II to save the Jews? Perhaps—but it's certain that no government, institution, of individual did as much as the Catholic Church under the leadership of Pius XII, and no attempt to rewrite history can change this fact.

Chapter 22:

Scandals and Schisms

Most historians agree that the most wicked or notorious of all the Popes was Alexander VI, who reigned from 1492-1503. The Spanish cardinal Rodrigo Borgia obtained the papacy by bribery; as Pope Alexander VI, he devoted himself a worldly and licentious lifestyle, while using the resources of the Church to provide for his nine children (born by six different women). Alexander was believed to have eliminated some of his enemies through the skillful use of poison; he himself died in that same manner after attending a banquet hosted by one of his cardinals.

A Catholic monk from Germany happened to visit Rome during Alexander's reign, and in his shock over the corruption he saw, wondered why God would allow such an evil and unfit person to preside over the Church. The monk's name was Martin Luther, and returning to Germany, he publicly protested against the many religious scandals and abuses he saw. This was a legitimate act on his part, and at first Luther truly sought nothing more than the reform of the Church. Over the next few years, however, his position hardened; he became less willing to compromise and discuss various issues, and—motivated in part by pride—Luther eventually revolted against the authority of the Church and began his own religious movement. As one recent convert from Protestantism to Catholicism noted, the Protestant Reformers "chose to deal with the problems in the 16th century Church, not by following the way of prayer and humility and the Cross, but by following the path of rebellion."[1]

During this same period of history, another man seeking religious truth decided to visit Rome. His Catholic friends tried to dissuade him, fearing he'd be so scandalized by what he saw he'd reject the Church, but the man insisted on going—and when he returned, he announced his new-found conviction that the Catholic Church was indeed the True Church founded by Christ. His relieved and amazed friends asked how he had come to this conclusion, and he responded, "Any Church still in existence after 1500 years, in spite of such widespread scandal and corruption, *has* to be protected and preserved by the Holy Spirit—there's no other possible explanation."

We can't control whether or not there are problems and even major scandals in the Church; what we *can* control is our response to the situation.

Because of human sinfulness, the Church is always in need of reform. This was true even at the very beginning; one of the Twelve Apostles, a man who spent three years in Christ's immediate company, ended up betraying Him, and the others ran away when their Master was arrested—with Peter, the leader of the Twelve (whom Jesus called the "Rock"), denying three times that he knew Him.

Even after the coming of the Holy Spirit on Pentecost Sunday, the early Christians weren't without sin; chapter 5 of the Acts of the Apostles describes how a Christian married couple—Ananias and Sapphira—tried to cheat the Church on a financial transaction. Our Lord's parable of the weeds among the wheat (Mt. 13:24-30) is a reminder that the Church would always contain sinful and even wicked members, mixed in with those truly seeking to travel the path of holiness. In that parable, Jesus warns us not to try to uproot or remove the weeds, but to leave the sorting out to God—at the moment and in the manner He chooses.

When times are especially difficult, God raises up great saints within the Church. One such saint was the holy bishop of Geneva, St. Francis de Sales, who lived in the difficult 16th and early 17th centuries. He was once asked about the scandalous example given by many bad priests of the day, and he said: "Those who commit these types of scandals are guilty of the spiritual equivalent of murder"—meaning they were destroying other people's faith in God by their bad example, and would surely be held accountable for that sin.

Then St. Francis added, "But I'm here among you to prevent something far worse for you. While those who give scandal are guilty of the spiritual equivalent of murder, those who *take* scandal—who allow scandals to destroy their faith—are guilty of spiritual suicide." In other words, leaving the Church because of the sinful behavior of some of her leaders and members is an act of cutting oneself off from the Sacraments—especially the Eucharist—and thereby depriving oneself of God's grace and interfering with His plan for one's life.

Author Ted Flynn writes, "At the hierarchical level, there has been an institutional stench and rot at all times in the history of the Church. It's simply the nature of man. The relative degree of health within the Church's clergy is typically a reflection of the nations they serve. When the clergy is silent [about the abuses of the day], Scripture tells us that they fail their job on the watchtower [cf. Ez. 33:1-9]. That is why when a nation is purified, it always starts first with the Church. This is precisely what we are seeing as scandals of a very serious nature consume today's clergy. The call today is the cry of Saint Francis de Sales, 'Do not commit spiritual suicide by tossing out what is good and holy because it has been abused by Judas.'"[2]

Archbishop Fulton J. Sheen once remarked that, given his choice, he preferred to live in times when the Church has suffered rather than thrived, times when the Church has to struggle and go against the culture. As he said, "Dead bodies float downstream, but it takes a real man, a real woman, to swim against the current." If our faith is built on the solid foundation of Christ Himself, it will be able to withstand the floods of scandal and schism.

There are people within the Church attempting to use these difficulties for their own purposes, claiming that the sexual abuse scandals prove the need for various changes—even when these so-called "reforms" go against Church doctrine or practice. Some of these dissenters are no doubt sincere and well-intentioned, but many others seem to have a less-than-honorable agenda. In the Letter to the Romans, St. Paul warns us, "I urge you, brothers, to watch out for those who cause divisions and put obstacles in your way that are contrary to the teaching you have learned. Keep away from them. For such people are not serving our Lord Jesus Christ, but their own appetites. By smooth talk and flattery they deceive the minds of naïve people" (16:17-18).

In his book *Call to Action or Call to Apostasy? How Dissenters Plan to Remake the Catholic Church in Their Own Image,* Dr. Brian Clowes (of the pro-life organization Human Life International) reveals the mindset of some of those persons agitating for major changes in Catholic doctrine and practice. When he asked persons attending a Call to Action national convention "Why do you stay in the Church?," the typical response was "To heal the Church of its many sins." The alleged sins being referred to, of course, were all of a corporate nature—racism, homophobia, sexism, and anti-Semitism—and not anything that would require a personal examination of conscience and conversion.

Dr. Clowes writes, "When the author asked CTA convention-goers the question 'What motivates you?,' they revealed the *true* reason that dissentters stay in the Church. They typically responded that 'The Church has absolutely no right to make us feel guilty about activities that our consciences tell us are moral.' . . . As long as the Roman Catholic Church exists in her current form, and as long as her teachings on moral issues remain inviolate, her very existence will be a rebuke to those committing immoral acts, and will cause them to feel guilty. So the dissenters' emphasis is not on personal repentance and sanctification, but the removal of the sensation of guilt while continuing and justifying their past and current behavior."[3]

The 2nd Letter of St. Peter warns us, "But there were also false prophets among the people; just as there will be false teachers among you. They will secretly introduce destructive heresies, even denying the sovereign Lord Who bought them—bringing swift destruction on themselves. Many will follow their shameful ways and will bring the way of truth into disrepute" (2:1-2).

St. Peter adds rather graphically, "It would have been better for them not to have known the way of righteousness, than to have known it and then to turn their backs on the sacred command that was passed on to them. Of them the proverbs are true: 'A dog returns to its vomit,' and 'A sow that is washed goes back to her wallowing in the mud'" (2:21-22).

As noted earlier, Pope Leo XIII had a vision in which the devil boasted that he could destroy the Catholic Church. That's what Satan is attempting to do, both from within and from without—but in that vision, Pope Leo also heard Jesus promise that the Church would emerge from this ordeal stronger and more beautiful than before. We can see the broad outlines of this struggle, and hints of the Church's coming triumph, as we look at the history of the last few centuries.

Chapter 23:

"Coincidences" in History

Our modern world is shaped by the Satanically-inspired events of three important years over the last few centuries: 1517, 1717, and 1917. Each of these years witnessed the beginning of a major assault on the unity and authority of the Catholic Church—and the effects are still being felt today.

1517 marked the beginning of the Protestant Reformation—or, more accurately, the Protestant Revolt. While there were many abuses in the Church needing correction, Martin Luther and the other "reformers" went much too far and ended up acting more out of pride than humility—and when that happens, the devil has an easier time taking over and twisting good intentions to serve his own evil purposes. Luther and his followers weren't all evil men, but they were unknowingly and unnecessarily serving an evil cause—for no one except Satan ultimately benefited from the division of the Church.

1717 was important because it marked the coming together of two ancient groups: a guild or professional organization of stonemasons, and a group of Satan-worshippers known as the Rosicrucians. On June 24, 1717, at the "Tavern of the Devil" in London, these two groups formally merged and formed the Grand Orient Lodge—more commonly known as Freemasonry. This new organization claimed that "Freemasonry alone possesses the true religion [Gnosticism]. All the other religions, especially Catholicism, have taken what is true in their doctrines from Freemasonry. They possess only false or absurd theories" (from Freemasonry's 1723 handbook *Free and Accepted Masons*).

The Catholic Church immediately condemned the Freemason's beliefs, and has continued doing so—more than 200 times. Catholics are still forbidden to belong to the Masons (a shortened form of the name Free-masons). Most Masons see only the good things or charitable activities their groups, or lodges, do; they're not allowed to discover the truth—namely, that their leaders are indirectly serving Satan, and that Masonry continues to oppose Christianity and especially the Catholic Church.[1]

Early in the 20th century, on the 200th anniversary of the founding of Freemasonry, the Masons and their supporters held a large and noisy parade in Rome, carrying banners showing Lucifer defeating St. Michael the Archangel—the exact opposite, of course, of what actually happened (cf. Rev. 12:7-9). The Masons made speeches attacking the Church—right outside St. Peter's Basilica . . . in the year 1917.

1917 was the year of the Russian Revolution, when the Communists came to power in Russia and began a murderous reign of terror against religion and against the Russian people as a whole. Communism represents one of Satan's worst assaults against humanity; it attacks every source of authority other than itself, and tramples human freedom, rights, and dignity in the process.

The two 19th century revolutionaries who are credited with founding Communism—Karl Marx and Friedrich Engels—were both Satanists. Marx, for instance, once wrote a poem titled *The Pale Maiden*, which said, "Thus heaven I've forfeited: I know it full well. My soul once true to God, is chosen for hell." In another poem, *The Prayer*, Marx writes: "The hellish vapors rise and fill the brain till I go mad and my heart is utterly changed. See this sword? The Prince of Darkness sold it to me; for he beats the time and gives the signs. Ever more boldly I play the dance of death."[2] Some scholars believe Marx and Engels themselves were both small pieces in a larger puzzle: namely, that Communism was actually created by the Masons, and other secret societies or groups working with them, as a means of gaining control of the world.[3]

There have been three major revolutions in modern world history: the American Revolution, the French Revolution, and the Russian Revolution. Only the American Revolution was truly successful and blessed by God; the patriots and colonists who fought for independence from Great Britain were, for the most part, dedicated Christians who honored the Lord—and for this reason, God blessed their efforts.

The Catholic Church looked with favor upon the American Revolution, but was steadfastly opposed to Communism from the very beginning. The Russian Revolution in 1917 helped make the 20th century the bloodiest in world history so far; tens of millions of innocent people—especially religious believers—have been murdered by the Communists (and this persecution continues in varying degrees in Communist countries such as China, North Korea, and Cuba).

The French Revolution of 1789, though not nearly as horrific as the Russian Revolution, was—in addition to being an assault on the French monarchy—also a major attack on the Church, and—contrary to popular belief, the lot of the common people worsened, rather than improved, as a result of the Revolution. Some scholars believe it too was partially organized or directed by the Masons. Ironically, the bloodshed, social upheaval, warfare, and religious persecution ushered in by the Revolution didn't have to happen; 100 years earlier Jesus offered a way to prevent it.

St. Margaret Mary Alacoque was a French religious sister to whom Jesus appeared a number of times (and it was to her that He expressed His desire that the Church promote devotion to His Sacred Heart). On June 17, 1689, Our Lord requested, through Sister Margaret Mary, that King Louis XIV consecrate France to the Sacred Heart of Jesus, promising that if the king did so and placed the image of the Sacred Heart on his banners and royal court of arms, He would give him eternal glory and victory over his enemies.

Louis XIV was a strong ruler (known to history as the "Sun King") but not a very moral or religious man, and he ignored Our Lord's request. A century later the French Revolution broke out, and King Louis XVI was deprived of his power by representatives of the Third Estate (the common people) on June 17, 1789—exactly 100 years to the day after Jesus' spurned offer.[4] Louis XVI was the opposite of Louis XIV—a weak leader, but a devout Catholic and a good man who truly cared for his people. He was executed by the guillotine several years later—showing that innocent people may suffer when God's requests are ignored. However, even when Heaven-sent opportunities are wasted, God always gives His people another chance.

This chance occurred in 1917; Jesus deliberately chose an important year in Satan's plan and upstaged the devil by sending His Mother to appear near a little town in Portugal named Fatima. On May 13 three children named Lucia, Jacinta, and Francisco, while tending their sheep, saw a luminous lady dressed in white. She told them to return to that spot on the 13th day of each month, and promised that in October, all who were present would see a great miracle. In her July apparition, Our Lady showed the children a vision of Hell, telling them to offer prayers and sacrifices for the conversion of sinners, and at different times, she made a number of predictions.

These predictions all came true: World War I ended the following year; Francisco and Jacinta both died while still children; a great evil—namely, Communism—came out of Russia and spread its errors and violence throughout the world; and the Holy Father had much to suffer. Mary also said that when Lucia saw the sky lit up one night by a great, unknown light, it would be a sign that a terrible new war was going to break out as a punishment for sin. However, Our Lady also gave a message of hope: if enough people prayed the Rosary, and if the Holy Father consecrated Russia to her Immaculate Heart, Russia would be converted and a period of peace would be given to the world. If people repented, Satan's plan—which had been underway for centuries—would be thwarted.

As described earlier (in Chapter 20), on October 13, 1917, the promised miracle occurred; 70,000 people witnessed what was called the "Dance of the Sun," in which the sun whirled about at a high rate of speed, changed colors, moved back and forth across the sky, and then appeared to plummet down to earth before resuming its normal position in the sky. The Catholic Church later investigated the apparitions at Fatima and declared them to be "worthy of belief." (Lucia herself went on to become a Carmelite religious sister, and lived until February 13, 2005.)

Many Catholics have taken the Fatima message very seriously, including the bishops of Portugal, who in 1931 consecrated their nation to the Immaculate Heart of Mary. As a result, Portugal was not involved in the terrible fighting of the Spanish Civil War, which broke out directly across her border in 1936, nor was she involved in World War II. Also, the Portuguese government, which had been bitterly anti-Catholic, was peacefully replaced by a new one which guaranteed the Church's freedom. Still another miracle was a vast increase in religious vocations; dioceses that had only a handful of priests, sisters, and seminarians in 1917 had much greater numbers only twenty years later. God's plan was to use Portugal as an example or demonstration of how nations could be blessed if only they turned back to Him and honored His Mother.

Mary had promised that a great, unknown light in the sky would foretell a coming war. This occurred in 1938 on the night of January 24-25. January 25 happens to be the feast of the conversion of St. Paul, who, as the early Church's great enemy Saul of Tarsus, was blinded by a great light as he approached Damascus. (It was also an "unknown" light, in the sense that Saul had to ask the Voice from Heaven, "Who are You, Sir?") On that date in 1938, the night skies over northern Europe were illuminated by a strange, eerie, beautiful red light, visible for thousands of miles. Sr. Lucia saw it from her convent window, and understood its meaning. As it happened, that same night a Polish nun, St. Faustina Kowalska, was given a vision of God's anger at Poland for the sins of her people. These events were indeed prophetic, for the following year, World War II began when Germany invaded Poland.

Chapter 24:

The Power of the Rosary

In chapter 6 of the Book of Revelation, the Lamb — Jesus — opens the seals on a scroll containing the meaning of all human history, thereby confirming the destiny of those who live in opposition to God. After the opening of the second seal, a fierce horseman emerged; he was given a huge sword, to use in spreading war throughout the earth. The color of this horseman was red (vv. 3-4). In 1938, following the appearance of an ominous red light across the night skies of northern Europe, Sr. Lucia sent a letter to her bishop in which she stated, "God made use of this to make me understand that His justice was about to strike the guilty nations."[1]

Scientists described the strange illumination as an *aurora borealis* of exceptional size and strength. (An aurora borealis, or northern lights, is a display of various forms and colors in the night sky — something rare, but not unknown.) However, Sr. Lucia later stated that "if scientists would investigate this aurora, they would find in the form in which it appeared, it was not and could not have been an aurora," and she added that one day a scientist would prove the truth of her words.

This in fact happened, though not until 1982. An American researcher studying records of the 1938 event discovered that it had produced almost exactly the same colors, patterns, and other phenomena as a nuclear explosion — including two giant red spots, which are not part of an aurora, but which can result from a nuclear detonation. Thus, even before nuclear weapons were invented, God was seemingly warning the world of a coming war in which these terrible devices would be used.

As we know, the first atomic bomb — in which a murderous explosion was accompanied by a blinding flash of light — was dropped on the Japanese city of Hiroshima on August 6, 1945. The date was perhaps symbolic, for August 6 is the Feast of the Transfiguration, when Jesus was seen by three of His apostles in the midst of a dazzling light. August 6 was also the date on which St. Dominic died in 1221, and it was to him that Our Lady had entrusted the Rosary as the weapon with which the Holy Trinity wants us to conquer the world.

As described in chapter 20, four Jesuit priests and four other Catholics were praying the Rosary in the Church of Our Lady of the Assumption, a mere eight blocks away from Ground Zero, when the atomic bomb was dropped—and not one of them was killed, injured, or even affected by radiation. The many scientists who examined them over the coming years had no medical or scientific explanations for this amazing fact. The same thing happened when a second atomic bomb was dropped on the city of Nagasaki three days later; a group of Franciscan friars who had been living the Fatima message of prayer and penance survived the blast and were also untouched by radiation.

The power of Jesus is infinitely stronger than any human weapons, even nuclear ones—and He has chosen to give His Mother a central role in protecting and guiding the Catholic Church through this most dangerous era of history. It's interesting that some of the most important dates of World War II occurred on Marian feast days. For instance, during the Battle of Britain in 1940, the Royal Air Force was fighting for its existence against the German *Luftwaffe*. After weeks of intense fighting, the British dealt a severe blow to the Germans, inflicting such heavy losses that a German invasion of England (which required aerial superiority) became untenable. The decisive date was September 15—the Feast of Our Lady of Sorrows.[2]

In 1941, the United States was drawn into the war when the Japanese attacked Pearl Harbor; America formally declared war on December 8—the Feast of the Immaculate Conception. Almost four years later, the U.S. tested the atomic bomb in the New Mexico desert before using it against the Japanese; the test occurred on July 16—the Feast of Our Lady of Mt. Carmel. The Japanese agreed to surrender a month later, on August 15— the Feast of the Assumption of Mary.

Other important events since World War II have also occurred on Marian feast days. Pope John Paul II was miraculously spared in an assassination attempt in 1981, which took place on May 13—the anniversary of Our Lady's first apparition at Fatima. (The Pope saw a girl in the crowd wearing a medal of Mary, and he bent down closer to her just as the bullet was fired—a movement that saved his life.) The Holy Father publicly credited Our Lady with sparing him. As time passed, the reason for this miracle became apparent: John Paul was Mary's chosen instrument in helping bring about the peaceful fall of Communism in Europe; his success in strengthening the Church and the labor union Solidarity in Poland set into motion an unexpected chain of events in Eastern Europe and the Soviet Union.

When Soviet hardliners attempted a 1991 coup or revolution against

Mikhail Gorbachev (under whose leadership the process of peaceful reform was occurring), they were defeated on August 22—the Feast of the Queenship of Mary. (The coup began on August 19, the anniversary of Mary's fourth apparition at Fatima—for the local authorities arrested the children prior to August 13 and imprisoned them for a few days, so as to prevent the apparition from occurring. That month Our Lady appeared to them six days later than usual, following their release.)

On December 8, 1991, the various republics of the Soviet Union formed a commonwealth, in which each one would be independent. A few weeks later, Gorbachev resigned as president of the Soviet Union. This occurred on December 25—Christmas Day, which celebrates Mary giving birth to Jesus. One week later, on January 1, 1992—the Solemnity of Mary as the Mother of God—the Soviet Union was formally dissolved.

Jesus is in control of the events of human history, and He has chosen His Mother as the "leading lady" in the drama that continues to unfold before our eyes. Mary, for her part, is urging—indeed, begging—all her children to do penance and to pray for peace in the world; in particular, she is asking us to help change the course of world events by praying the Rosary.

There are numerous historical examples of the Rosary's power. In the 12th century St. Dominic was struggling to convert the Albigensians, a group of former Christians who had fallen into heresy. Dominic had virtually no success—until Our Lady appeared to him and taught him to pray and promote the Rosary. From then on, his efforts bore great fruit.

In 1474, the German city of Cologne was miraculously saved from an enemy attack once the people there prayed the Rosary for this intention. An even greater threat was faced by Catholic Europe in 1571; a powerful Turkish fleet was poised to seize control of the Mediterranean Sea, opening up southern Europe to invasion. Even as the Catholic nations hastily assembled a fleet to meet the threat, Pope St. Pius V urged all members of the Church to pray the Rosary. As a result, at the Battle of Lepanto on October 7, the Christian fleet miraculously defeated the invaders (and afterwards, the Church began observing October 7 as the Feast of the Most Holy Rosary).

Even in our modern world the Rosary has made a difference. At the end of World War II, the Soviet Union occupied all of Eastern Europe, including the eastern half of the Catholic nation of Austria. The Cold War between the Soviet Union and the United States and its allies was underway, and the Soviets stubbornly refused to give up any of the territory they had conquered. Austria in particular was a key strategic position (Napoleon had called it the key to dominating Europe), and the Russians had no intention of leaving. Beginning in 1948, tens of thousands of Austrians committed themselves to praying the Rosary every day until the Soviet Army left their homeland. It took seven years, but in 1955, without any warning and without demanding anything in return, the Soviets suddenly evacuated eastern Austria, thereby restoring the nation's unity and freedom. The date on which this occurred was May 13.

Also in 1948, Joseph Cardinal Mindszenty, the leader of the Catholic Church in Hungary—in his last sermon before being imprisoned by the Communists—said, "Give me a million families with rosaries in their hands, uplifted to Mary. They will be a military power, not against other people, but for all mankind. . . . With [the Rosary] in our hands, we shall conquer ourselves, convert sinners, do penance for our country, and will certainly move the merciful, mild, and benevolent Heart of Mary." The Cardinal's prophecy was fulfilled just over forty years later, in the peaceful revolution of 1989 (200 years after the bloody French Revolution).

In 1964, with the connivance of its left-wing government, Brazil was on the verge of being taken over by the Communists. The Archbishop of Rio de Janeiro warned his countrymen in a radio address of what was happening, and begged them to respond to Our Lady's requests at Fatima. As a result, a nationwide Rosary crusade was begun, with hundreds of thousands of women marching in prayer—and the crisis was ended. Inspired by these huge, peaceful prayer rallies, the army launched a preemptive coup against the traitorous government, thereby preserving the nation's liberty.

It is believed that the intervention of Our Lady has helped prevent nuclear war on at least two occasions. In October 1960, Nikita Khrushchev, the Soviet leader, visited the United Nations in New York and boasted that the Soviet Union "would bury" the West. Khrushchev's confidence was based on knowledge that Soviet scientists were working on an advanced nuclear missile, which was only weeks away from completion. In response to the crisis, the Bishop of Fatima—at the request of Pope John XXIII— wrote to all the Catholic bishops of the world and invited them and their people to spend a night of prayer for world peace on October 12-13 (the anniversary of the final Fatima apparition). At Fatima itself, a million Catholics gathered to pray the Rosary before the Blessed Sacrament. That very night, the Soviets were testing their new weapon, but something went drastically wrong, and an explosion killed 300 of their top military leaders and scientists—setting their nuclear missile program back twenty years and preventing a possible nuclear war.

On March 25, 1984 (the Feast of the Annunciation), Pope John Paul II consecrated the world the Immaculate Heart of Mary—an act which Sr. Lucia later said prevented a nuclear war that would have otherwise occurred the following year. On May 13, 1984, a large crowd was praying the Rosary at Fatima. A few hours later a gigantic explosion occurred in the weapons storage area for the Soviets' largest and most powerful fleet; two-thirds of its surface-to-air and ship-to-ship missiles were wiped out in the greatest disaster experienced by the Soviet Navy since World War II, making it impossible for the Soviet Union to launch a war at that time. Exactly four years later, as thousands prayed the Rosary all night long at Fatima on the eve of the anniversary of Our Lady's first apparition there, an explosion shut down the only factory in Russia capable of producing motors for the Soviet's most powerful nuclear missile.[3]

Our Lady is said to have revealed to a contemporary priest the power and importance of the Rosary:

> By this prayer, you offer your Heavenly Mother a powerful force in intervening for the salvation of many of my poor straying children. . . . Your entire Rosary is like an immense chain of love and salvation with which you are able to encircle persons and situations, and *even to influence all the events of your time* [emphasis added]. . . The Rosary is the prayer which I myself came down from Heaven to ask of you. By it you are able to lay bare the plots of my adversary; you escape from many of his deceits; you defend yourselves from many dangers which he puts in your way; it preserves you from evil and brings you even closer to me, because I am able to be truly your guide and protection.[4]

According to St. Josemaría Escrivá, "The Rosary is a powerful weapon. Use it with confidence and you will be amazed at the results." Our Lady wants us, by means of prayer and penance, to cooperate in her efforts to lead sinners back to her Son Jesus, and to bring about true peace in the world. She is the Heavenly Mother, not only of Catholics, but of all who love her Son, and she offers us her assistance and protection in times of danger. Therefore, in the words of St. Francis de Sales, "Let us run to her, and, as her little children, cast ourselves into her arms with a perfect confidence."

Chapter 25:

Looking to the Church's Future Triumph

Ten years before his 1941 martyrdom in Auschwitz, St. Maximilian Kolbe, a Franciscan priest with a deep devotion to Mary, wrote: "The serpent raises his head over the whole earth, but the Immaculate is going to crush him through decisive victories, although he does not cease to lie in wait for her Heel [cf. Gen. 3:15]. Under the standard of the Immaculate a great battle will be waged, and we shall have her banners float over the fortresses of the prince of darkness."

Elaborating on this compelling theme, St. Maximilian continued,

> Then heresies and schisms will be extinguished, and hardened sinners, thanks to the Immaculate, will return to God, toward His Heart full of love, and all pagans will be baptized. Thus will be accomplished what the blessed Saint Catherine Labouré—to whom the Immaculate revealed the Miraculous Medal—had foretold: that is that the Immaculate will become "the Queen of the whole world" and "of each one in particular."[1]

This prophecy echoes Our Lady's words at Fatima, where she announced that "In the end, my Immaculate Heart will triumph," and promised that a period of peace would be given to the world.

Devotion to the Immaculate Heart of Mary is widely recognized as an important Catholic practice—though many people are unaware of its solid scriptural foundation. We read in the Gospel of Luke that after the visit of the shepherds to the newborn King outside Bethlehem, "Mary kept all these things, reflecting on them in her heart" (2:19). Soon after this, when Mary and Joseph presented the child Jesus at the Temple in fulfillment of the Law of Moses, the prophet Simeon—inspired by the Holy Spirit—told Mary that a sword of sorrow would pierce her heart (2:35). Twelve years later, after finding the young Jesus in the Temple following a search of three days, "His mother kept all these things in her heart" (2:51), continuing to reflect on her role in God's plan of salvation while constantly renewing her commitment to live as His faithful handmaid (cf. Lk. 1:38).

Many Catholic saints and mystics in the Middle Ages, including St. Anselm, St. Bernard, St. Gertrude the Great, and St. Brigid of Sweden, practiced devotion to the Immaculate Heart of Mary,[2] but it's in recent times that this devotion has taken on special importance. Our Lady's apparitions at Fatima emphasized Christ's desire that His Mother be honored, particularly in her Immaculate Heart, and in 1942—a little over one year after the heroic death of St. Maximilian Kolbe (who offered his life in exchange for that of another condemned prisoner)—Pope Pius XII consecrated the world to the Immaculate Heart of Mary. This act occurred when Nazi Germany was at the height its power, but immediately after this, the tide of the war turned; indeed, Jesus later revealed to a Sr. Lucia that World War II was shortened as a result of the Pope's action.[3]

The Catholic Church has never doubted the power of prayer, particularly when it involves asking for the intercession of the Blessed Virgin Mary on our behalf. From the very beginning of her Son's public ministry—at the wedding feast in Cana—she intervened on behalf of those in need (Jn. 2:1-11), and it pleases Our Lord to grant her requests for her children on earth. Moreover, that His Mother might be even more highly honored, Jesus has chosen to grant victory to His Church and peace to the world through her ongoing heavenly intercession.

Because of original sin (which we inherited from Adam and Eve) and our own personal sinfulness, true and lasting peace cannot come about through human efforts alone. As the *Catechism* teaches, "Earthly peace is the image and fruit of the *peace of Christ*, the messianic 'Prince of Peace.' By the blood of His Cross, 'in His own person He killed the hostility [Eph. 2:16], he reconciled men with God and made His Church the sacrament of the unity of the human race and of its union with God" (par. 2305).

In spite of the many religious conflicts in human history (including religiously motivated wars and terrorism in today's world), all religions at the very least claim to desire peace—but only Christianity can offer that true peace which this world cannot give (cf. Jn. 14:27). Even more specifically, only Catholicism can offer the fullness of Christ's peace through the leadership and Sacraments of His Church. Moreover, it's only Catholicism that God has chosen to entrust with the "Peace Plan from Heaven": repentance, sacrifice and penance, prayer (especially the Rosary), devotion to the Mother of God, and consecration (particularly of Russia) to her Immaculate Heart.

Many Catholic visionaries and saints—including St. John Vianney, St. Francis of Paola, Bl. Anna Maria Taigi, and Bl. Johannes Amadeus de Sylva, among others—have spoken of a coming era of peace, a time of triumph for the Catholic Church and of blessing and prosperity for all humanity.[4] Sister Mary of Agreda (d. 1665), for instance, stated:

> It was revealed to me that through the intercession of the Mother of God all heresies will disappear. This victory over heresies has been reserved by Christ for His Blessed Mother. In the last times the Lord will especially spread the renown of His Mother: Mary began salvation and by her intercession it will be concluded. Before the second coming of Christ Mary must, more than ever, shine in mercy, might and grace in order to bring unbelievers into the Catholic Faith. The powers of Mary in the last times over the demons will be very conspicuous. Mary will extend the reign of Christ over the heathens and Mohammedans and it will be a time of great joy when Mary, as Mistress and Queen of Hearts, is enthroned.[5]

Similarly, St. Louis de Montfort (d. 1716) predicted that Mary "will extend the Kingdom of Christ over the idolaters and Moslems, and there will come a glorious era in which Mary will be the ruler and Queen of human hearts."

When will this glorious era of peace and religious unity begin, and how will it arrive in our grievously wounded world?

No once can say with certainty, but—according to students of Catholic prophecy—there can be no doubt that such an age will occur. (This coming era of peace is not to be confused with the Millennium, or 1000 year reign of Christ, described in the Book of Revelation.[6]) It greatly pleases Our Lord to give His Mother a central role in His coming triumph, and to reward His Church for her fidelity to her mission in spite of the opposition of the world. This, then, can be seen as a final reason for becoming or remaining Catholic: the opportunity to share as fully as possible in Jesus' coming victory here on earth, and the absolute certainty of entering His Kingdom by means of the Sacraments and spiritual resources His Church provides.

The scroll given to the Lamb in chapter 5 of the Book of Revelation represents God's plan for history; this plan is entrusted to Jesus, the Lamb—and He, in turn, has chosen to bring about His triumph through the intercession of His Mother and the faithful endurance and witness of His Church (cf. Rev. 5:1-10; 7:9-14; 12:1-6, 13-17; 19:5-9). You and I are called to play our part in this ongoing plan of salvation through personal repentance, the fulfillment of our spiritual duties, and especially through our prayers.

Prayer is the most powerful force on earth—and it is the Catholic Church, more than any other, which believes and promotes this truth. Jesus and Mary are working through the Church in a powerful way, and they are begging each of us to do our part in helping bring about peace and save sinners from eternal damnation.

At Fatima and at many other sites of alleged apparitions, Our Lady has asked us to repent of our own sins, to do penance and to pray for world peace and the conversion of sinners. In particular, we're asked to pray the Rosary. Some Protestants pray the Rosary, and that's a wonderful thing—but it's the Catholic Church to which Heaven has entrusted this prayer, and we as Catholics must take up this powerful weapon.

Jesus Christ is the Lord of all history; nothing can happen against His Divine Will, and nothing can do lasting harm to His Church or to those who trust in Him. He is actively involved in the unfolding of world events; He may allow disasters or suffering to occur to certain nations or peoples as punishment for their sins and as a reminder of their need for Him, but those who repent and turn back to Him will certainly be saved.

The "coincidences" we see in history are actually signs that God's plan is unfolding. The Lord respects our free will, but then He weaves all our choices—whether good or bad—into His ongoing design. Every Christian is invited to be part of this process of redemption, and the safest and most powerful way of doing so is by our active membership in the One, Holy, Catholic, and Apostolic Church.

NOTES

Chapter 2

1   The Coming Home Network is an apostolate run by lay persons (including Marcus Grodi, a former Protestant minister who converted to Catholicism) offering information, encouragement, and support to Protestants—especially clergy—seriously considering conversion to Catholicism. For information, write to The Coming Home Network, P.O. Box 8290, Zanesville, OH 43702-8290, or call (740) 450-1175.

2   Rev. Alex Jones, "Return to Apostolic Traditions," *This Rock* (July-August 2000), pp. 27-31.

Chapter 3

1   *Surprised by Truth: 11 Converts Give the Biblical and Historical Reasons for Becoming Catholic* (Basilica Press, 1994). Since the first book came out, Mr. Madrid has added two more: *Surprised by Truth 2* (Sophia Institute Press, 2000), and *Surprised by Truth 3* (Sophia Institute Press, 2002).

2   Rick Conason, *Surprised by Truth,* p. 176.

3   Julie Swenson, *Surprised by Truth,* p. 155.

4   Dave Armstrong, *Surprised by Truth,* p. 246.

5   Ibid., p. 248.

6   Steve Wood, *Surprised by Truth,* p. 87.

7   David Currie, *Born Fundamentalist, Born Again Catholic* (Ignatius, 1996), p. 100.

8   Scott Hahn, *The Lamb's Supper* (Doubleday, 1999), pp. 7-8.

9   Ibid., pp. 119-120.

Chapter 4

1   Joan Carroll Cruz, *Angels & Devils* (TAN Books & Publishing), p. 219.

2   Ibid., p. 223.

3   Ibid., pp. 234-35.

4   Ibid., pp. 236-37.

Chapter 5

1   This chapter is based on my article "Christian Yes, But Why Catholic?" in the October 1999 issue of *This Rock*.

Chapter 7

1   James Akin, *Surprised by Truth*, p. 66.

Chapter 8

1   John Stoddard, *Rebuilding A Lost Faith* (TAN), pp. 136-37.

Chapter 10

1   Steve Wood, *Surprised by Truth*, p. 89.

2   Scott Butler, et al., *Jesus, Peter & the Keys* (Queenship, 1996), p.12ff.

Chapter 12

1   *Surprised by Truth*, p. 88.

Chapter 13

1   Rev. G. E. Howe, *Stories from the Catechist* (TAN, 1898), pp. 79-80.

Chapter 19

1   See, for instance, my books *Saintly Solutions to Life's Common Problems* (Sophia Institute Press, 2001), and *More Saintly Solutions to Life's Common Problems* (Sophia Institute Press, 2004).

Chapter 20

1   Numerous examples are given in two books by Joan Carroll Cruz: *Mysteries, Marvels, & Miracles in the Lives of the Saints* (TAN, 1997), and *Miraculous Images of Our Lady* (TAN, 1993). See also *Raised from the Dead: True Stories of 400 Resurrection Miracles*, by Fr. Albert J. Hebert, S. M. (TAN, 1986).

Chapter 21

1   Two excellent histories of the Church are *Triumph: The Power and the Glory of the Catholic Church,* by H. W. Crocker III (Three Rivers Press, 2001), and *Christ the King: Lord of History,* by Anne W. Carroll (TAN, 1994).

2   Material in this section is based on *How the Catholic Church Built Western Civilization,* by Thomas E. Woods, Jr. (Regnery, 2005).

3   *Christ the King: Lord of History,* p. 235.

4   *Triumph: The Power and the Glory of the Catholic Church,* pp. 236-37.

5   Material in this section is based on the booklet *Why Apologize for the Spanish Inquisition?,* by Very Rev. Alphonsus Maria Duran, M. J. (Miles Jesu, 2000).

6   Material in this section is based on *Hitler, the War, and the Pope,* by Ronald Rychlak (Our Sunday Visitor, 2000), and *Pius XII and the Holocaust: A Reader* (The Catholic League for Religious and Civil Liberties, 1988).

Chapter 22

1   Julie Swenson, *Surprised by Truth,* p. 135.

2   Ted Flynn, *Idols in the House* (MaxKol Communications, 2002), p. 249.

3   Dr. Brian Clowes, *Call to Action or Call to Apostasy?* (Human Life International, 1997), pp. 21-22.

Chapter 23

1   Further information on this point may be found in *Their God is the Devil: Papal Encyclicals and Freemasonry,* by Paul A. Fisher (American Research Foundation, 1991), and *She Shall Crush Thy Head,* by Stephen Mahowald (MMR Publishing, 1996). For a non-Catholic perspective on the dangers of Masonry, see *The Dark Side of Freemasonry,* edited by Ed Decker (Huntington House, 1994).

2   *She Shall Crush Thy Head,* p. 108.

3   Ibid., p. 105ff.

4   Thomas W. Petrisko, *The Fatima Prophecies* (St. Andrew's Publications, 1998), p. 76.

Chapter 24

1   Ted and Maureen Flynn, *The Thunder of Justice* (MaxKol Communications, 1993), p.139.

2   Professor Courtney Bartholomew, *The Last Help Before the End of Time* (Queenship, 2006 revised edition), p. 75.

3   Rev. Albert Shamon, *Preparing for the Third Millennium* (The Riehle

Foundation, 1996), pp. 19-21.

4   Message of October 7, 1979 to Fr. Stefano Gobbi, in *To the Priests, Our Lady's Beloved Sons* (Marian Movement of Priests, 1995).

Chapter 25

1   Frère François de Marie des Anges, *Fatima: Prophecies of Tragedy and Triumph*, Book Four (Immaculate Heart Publications, 1994), p. 312.

2   Anthony F. Chiffolo, *100 Names of Mary* (St. Anthony Messenger Press, 2002), p. 33.

3   Diane Moczar, *Ten Dates Every Catholic Should Know* (Sophia Institute Press, 2005), p. 168.

4   Other such visionaries include Ven. Bartholomew Holzhauser, Sister Jeanne de Royer, the Ecstatic of Tours, Telesphorus of Cozensa, Abbot Joachim, Fr. Laurence Ricci, Brother John of the Cleft Rock, Joseph Goires, and Sister Marie Lataste. For more information on this subject, see Desmond Birch's *Trial, Tribulation & Triumph* (Queenship, 1996), and my own *After the Darkness* (Queenship, 1997).

5   Edward Connor, *Prophecy for Today* (Apostolate of Christian Action, 1956), p. 45.

6   Unlike many Fundamentalists and other Bible Christians, the Catholic Church does not interpret the 1000-year period mentioned in Rev. 20:1-6 as a literal earthly reign of Christ. Rather, ever since the time of St. Augustine, the Church has seen this passage as generally referring to the period of human History between Christ's First and Second Comings.

RECOMMENDED READING

After the Darkness: A Novel on the Coming of the Antichrist and the End of the World, Rev. Joseph M. Esper (Queenship, 1997).

Answer Me This, Patrick Madrid (Our Sunday Visitor).

Answering a Fundamentalist, Rev. Albert J. Nevins (Our Sunday Visitor).

Born Fundamentalist, Born Again Catholic, David B. Currie (Ignatius, 1996).

Catholic Apologetics Today: Answers to Modern Critics, Rev. William C. Most (TAN Books & Publishers, 1986).

Catholicism and Fundamentalism, Karl Keating (Ignatius Press, 1988).

Confessions of a Roman Catholic, Paul Whitcomb (TAN Books & Publishers, 1958).

Crossing the Tiber: Evangelical Protestants Discover the Historical Church, Stephen K. Ray (Ignatius, 1997).

Handbook of Christian Apologetics, Peter Kreeft and Ronald Tacelli, S. J. (Ignatius Press).

How Not to Share Your Faith: The Seven Deadly Sins of Catholic Apologists And Evangelization, Mark Brumley (Catholic Answers).

How the Catholic Church Built Western Civilization, Thomas E. Woods, Jr. (Regnery, 2005).

Journeys Home, Marcus Grodi (Queenship, 1997).

Rome Sweet Home, Scott & Kimberly Hahn (Ignatius, 1993).

Scripture Alone? 21 Reasons to Reject 'Sola Scriptura,' Joel Peters (TAN Books & Publishers, 1999).

Strangers at Your Door: How to Respond to Jehovah Witnesses, the Mormons, Televangelists, Cults, and More, Rev. Albert J. Nevins (Our Sunday Visitor).*Surprised by Truth,* ed. by Patrick Madrid (Basilica Press, 1994).

Surprised by Truth 2, ed. by Patrick Madrid (Sophia Institute Press,

2000).

Surprised by Truth 3, ed. by Patrick Madrid (Sophia Institute Press, 2002).

Ten Reasons to Come Back to the Catholic Church, Lorene Hanley Duquin (Our Sunday Visitor).

The Catholic Church Has the Answer, Paul Whitcomb (TAN Books & Publishers, 1986).

The Lamb's Supper, Scott Hahn (Doubleday, 1999).

The Last Help Before the End of Time, Prof. Courtney Bartholomew (Queenship, revised 2nd edition, 2006).

The Thunder of Justice, Ted and Maureen Flynn (MaxKol Communications,1993).

The Usual Suspects: Answering Anti-Catholic Fundamentalists, Karl Keating (Ignatius Press, 2000).

There We Stood, Here We Stand: 11 Lutherans Rediscover their Catholic Roots, ed. by Timothy Drake (1st Books Library, 2001).

Trial, Tribulation & Triumph, Desmond A. Birch (Queenship, 1996).

12 Painless Ways to Evangelize, Karl Keating (Catholic Answers, 1995).

When A Loved One Leaves the Church, Lorene Hanley Duquin (Our Sunday Visitor).

Where Is That In the Bible?, Patrick Madrid (Our Sunday Visitor, 2001).

Where We Got the Bible: Our Debt to the Catholic Church, Rt. Rev. Henry G. Graham (TAN Books & Publishers, 1911, 30th reprinting 2004).

Why is That in Tradition?, Patrick Madrid (Our Sunday Visitor).